Everest
The Unclimbed Ridge

Chris Bonington, 48, is one of Britain's leading climbers who has made many new routes in the UK and the European Alps and expeditions to the Himalaya and Karakoram regularly since 1960. In 1970 he led the first great face climb of an 8000-metre peak, Annapurna South Face, and in 1975 led the first successful ascent of the South West Face of Everest. His most recent climbing has been in China, described in *Kongur, China's Elusive Summit*. His recent books also include *Everest the Hard Way* and *Quest For Adventure*. He holds the Founder's Medal of the Royal Geographical Society.

Charles Clarke, 39, is Consultant Neurologist at St. Bartholomew's Hospital and Whipps Cross Hospital, London, and had been on seven Himalayan expeditions before being invited to join the 1975 Everest South West Face expedition as medical officer. Six years later he was part of the four-man scientific team which went with the climbers to Mount Kongur, and has been engaged in research on the effects of oxygen lack at high altitude. He is Honorary Medical Officer to the British Mountaineering Council.

Also by Chris Bonington
in Pan Books

Quest for Adventure

Everest
The Unclimbed Ridge

Chris Bonington and Charles Clarke

Pan Books London and Sydney

First published 1983 by Hodder and Stoughton Ltd
This edition published 1984 by Pan Books Ltd,
Cavaye Place, London SW10 9PG
9 8 7 6 5 4 3 2 1
© Jardine, Matheson & Co Ltd 1983
ISBN 0 330 28497 5
Photoset by Parker Typesetting Service, Leicester
Printed in Great Britain by
Richard Clay (The Chaucer Press) Ltd, Bungay, Suffolk

To Pete and Joe

Authors' note

A library on Everest already exists, recording many attempts, successes, failures and tragedies. In adding to this we record the story of a small expedition, pieced together from our own thoughts and memories and the diaries of those who kept them. We are indebted to Hilary Boardman for allowing us to use Peter's diary freely, and to Maria Coffey for Joe's letters.

Chris Bonington/Charles Clarke
May 1983

Contents

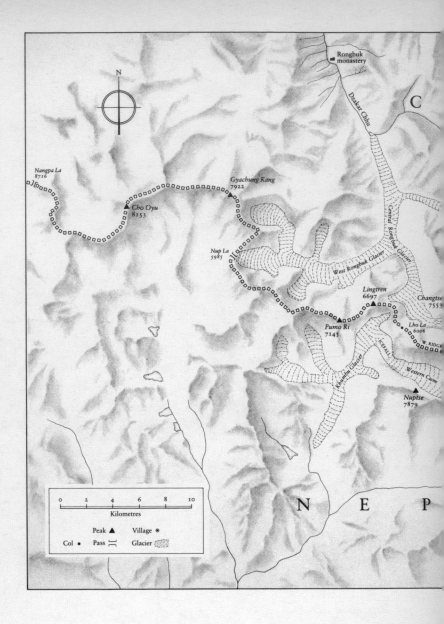

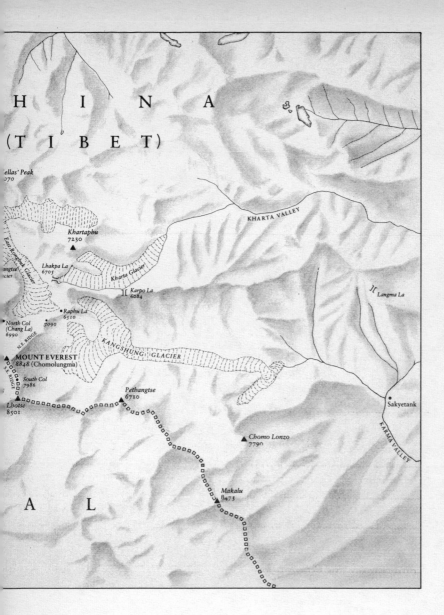

C H I N A

(T I B E T)

ellas' Peak
070

Khartaphu
7230 ▲

KHARTA VALLEY

East Rongbuk Glacier

Lhakpa La
6705

Kharta Glacier

angtse
cier

Karpo La
6084

Langma La

• *Raphu La*
6510

• North Col
(Chang La)
6990

7090

KANGSHUNG GLACIER

N.E. RIDGE

▲ **MOUNT EVEREST**
8848 (Chomolungma)

• Sakyetank

S.E. RIDGE

South Col
7986

Pethangtse
6710 ▲

Lhotse
8501

KARMA VALLEY

▲ *Chomo Lonzo*
7790

A   L

Makalu
8475 ▲

1: 'A worthwhile objective'

April 1981–1st March 1982/Charles Clarke

'You *are* coming to Everest next year, aren't you?' was how Chris put it. It was the first I knew of it. It was April 1981 and we were spending the weekend at the Glenridding Hotel on the shores of Ullswater in preparation for the 1981 British Mount Kongur Expedition to China. While we talked logistics and tested tents, filmed and held a press conference, I sensed that our meeting had two roles. Its overt purpose was to plan our visit to Mount Kongur on the southern border of Xinjiang, China's western province: more surreptitiously, the seeds were sown for the first British expedition to the Tibetan side of Everest for over forty years. Peter Boardman, Al Rouse, Joe Tasker and I slipped off downstairs on the Sunday morning to hear Chris unfurl the plans to attempt the little known North East Ridge of Everest from Tibet the following year.

The highest mountain in the world lies between two Himalayan nations, a giant pyramid astride the frontier of Nepal and Tibet. Its southern flank, bounded by the West Ridge and the South East Ridge, lies in Nepal and has been visited extensively since the second world war. The Tibetan side is at present less well known but was explored thoroughly by British expeditions in the 1920s and '30s. Between the 3000-metre East, or Kangshung Face, and the north wall of the mountain lies the North East Ridge, three miles long. Unclimbed, obvious, long and elegant as a route, it was a magnificent virgin line, the only ridge left for a new route on Everest. Thus it remains.

It is often difficult to explain the choice of a route on a mountain. If the peak is unknown or unclimbed there seems little need to justify the intention to attempt a first ascent. For second and subsequent ascents of peaks above 8000 metres, such is the scale of the undertaking that the choice becomes of crucial importance. Why, for example, was it more attractive to us to attempt the North East Ridge of Everest from Tibet rather than an unclimbed route on Lhotse, Everest's 8500-metre neighbour, from Nepal? First, geographical innovation makes a route attractive. Nepal, whilst being a fascinating, hospitable and delightful country, is now very much on the tourist routes of the Far East, with Kathmandu connected by frequent flights to several Indian cities and to Bangkok. Kathmandu with its quaint Hindu charm is no longer a place few Europeans have visited. All of us had been to the Himalaya during the previous fifteen years on several occasions – we once calculated we had been on over forty expeditions between us – and had cast longing glances to the northern border of Nepal, to Tibet, the forbidden land under Chinese rule. In the late 1970s, in keeping with the change of policy in the People's Republic of China, Tibet was, for the first time in forty years, becoming a country a foreigner could visit. First a few privileged invited guests were taken to Lhasa, the capital, and Xigaze and Gyantse, central Tibet's major towns. The writer Han Suyin described her visit in 1975, and, in her view, the great improvements in the country since the Chinese had taken over in 1950. A few tourists were allowed to visit in 1978 and 1979 and in that year an event took place which was to revolutionise mountaineering in Central Asia.

With little warning to outsiders, though with great internal preparation, in October 1979 the Chinese government opened selected high mountains to foreign expeditions. Great peaks which had almost disappeared into climbing mythology could once again be reached; within months of the announcement teams from Europe, the United States and Japan were deep in conference with the officials of the Chinese Mountaineering Association in Peking. In addition to Chomolungma (Mount Everest), 8848 metres, there were Xixabangma, 8012 metres, in Tibet, Anyemaqen, 6282 metres, in Qinghai Province, Gongga (Minya Konka), 7566 metres, and Siguniang, 6250 metres, in Sichuan Province, Bogda, 5445 metres, Mustagh Ata, 7549 metres, Kongur Tiube, 7595 metres, and Mount Kongur, 7719 metres, in Xinjiang Province. Each of these mountains was geographically very attractive to a small group of climbers and high-altitude scientists who had come together under the leadership of Michael Ward, a London surgeon and veteran Himalayan climber from the 1950s and early '60s. At the time, in the early months of 1980, we chose Mount Kongur, an almost unknown peak in the far west of Xinjiang. In 1980 Kongur was one of the highest unclimbed peaks in the world, in a forgotten corner of Central Asia. It satisfied the instinct in all of us for exploration, to attempt to climb a very high, almost unknown peak and to mount a high-altitude scientific expedition. The story of *Kongur, China's Elusive Summit*[1] has already been told and on this happy and successful expedition we explored the Kongur massif, the only mountain group on the 'Chinese List' which still seemed surrounded with an air of mystery. How we longed for more peaks to be available.

For a second expedition to China within the confines of the bureaucratic rules, the North East Ridge of Everest was an obvious choice. An approach through Tibet would be intriguing and whilst in the Everest region we would be following routes explored by the British expeditions which visited the Tibetan side of the mountain between the two world wars. The Ridge itself was elegant, unknown and looked, from the few photographs we had, difficult but possible. The route of our choice had to satisfy one other, purely self-imposed, criterion. It had to be climbable by a small expedition without high-altitude porters and without oxygen. There were alternatives on Everest, for example an attempt on the Kangshung Face on its eastern

[1]*Kongur, China's Elusive Summit*, Chris Bonington, Hodder & Stoughton, 1982.

side. We rejected this – the route seemed too dangerous because of avalanches. There are other firsts to be done on Everest (though it has been climbed alone, alone without oxygen, at night and by at least six different routes). One colossal undertaking would be a traverse of the mountain from Nepal to Tibet and doubtless one day this will be done.

If Everest were to be the successor to Kongur there was one catalyst essential to both ventures – money. Through a stroke of genius, luck and excellent advice, Michael Ward and Chris Bonington had met David Newbigging, Chairman of one of Hong Kong's greatest companies, Jardine, Matheson & Co., Ltd. Jardines, originally a Scots trading company, was established in the Far East just over 150 years ago and now has not only a large financial stake in the prosperity of Hong Kong but links with China which, though established in Chinese Imperial days, have lasted (with some hiccups) through the changes of the Kuomintang, Civil War, Liberation and Cultural Revolution. Jardines agreed first to underwrite the Kongur Expedition and showed interest in Chris Bonington's proposals for Everest. Without them it is doubtful whether either expedition could have taken place but with them there was finance on generous terms, a deep knowledge and understanding of China and their own managers, agents and friends in many of the principal Chinese cities.

While we travelled across China to Kongur in May 1981, accompanied by David Newbigging and a small group of Jardines' personnel, we discussed the plans for Everest. Thus before Kongur was even attempted, we had a loose agreement that Everest might be a going concern. Martin Henderson, Financial Director of Mathesons, their London-based company, had taken to climbing and expedition organisation with enthusiasm. 'It's certainly a worthwhile objective,' he said, slipping into climbing jargon. For many multi-national companies could there be anything *less* 'worthwhile' than sending six men to Tibet to climb a mountain?

It seemed odd to be travelling across China in 1981, to a remote part of Xinjiang and to be already discussing the next expedition, but such is the pace of modern Himalayan climbing and the insistence by the Chinese for clearly defined plans that we needed to have made firm arrangements for the following year before returning to Britain.

Kongur taught us many things. Visits to mountains within the People's Republic are experiences very different from trips to the southern Himalaya. The Chinese love order and insist upon precise logistic details, such as bookings for trucks, jeeps, porters and yaks well in advance. The weight of expedition administration, the time-consuming arguments with customs officials, airlines, Sherpas and porters, do not, or should not, exist in China. Superficially this is very attractive for an expedition is almost guaranteed to reach its mountain on time and in good order. Experience on Kongur had taught us how efficient this system could be – but how well organised we needed to be to take advantage of it. My only reservation was that such relentless efficiency lacked a little of the familiar charm and chaos of many a southern Himalayan scene and also that China is grotesquely expensive for foreigners.

On Kongur, we had made very real friends in China. Mr Shi Zhanchun, Vice-Chairman of the Chinese Mountaineering Association, who had himself led two successful Everest expeditions, went out of his way to help us, advising us in detail about logistics in southern Tibet. Our relationship with Jardines, too, had matured. We had grown to understand each other and real friendships had formed. David Newbigging, a man of immense personal charisma and power had, it seemed, taken to the climbing scene, to our unruly dress in the immaculate air conditioned offices of Hong Kong and the curious aspirations of mountaineers, so different from the material dedication of the Jardines' empire. Relationships between a team and its sponsors are beset with potential difficulties; whilst recognising with immense gratitude the financial backing from any organisation, an expedition needs to feel that it is itself the master of its destiny. Though as dependent as an infant, a team does not want to be dominated by the Great Provider. Jardines sensed this almost instinctively and gave us freedom. In turn we felt we behaved towards the company with a filial loyalty without feeling that we were under coercion to act unnaturally in the many public and private engagements we shared. A good example of this were the trekking parties of non-climbers organised by Jardines which accompanied us happily on both expeditions as far as Base Camp and explored with us until we acclimatised. In the sense that after a liaison of three years we are still firm friends, the relationship has been very successful and certainly without Jardines' backing, successive instalments of the 1980 Kongur Reconnaissance, the 1981 Kongur Expedition and this Everest Expedition would have been a very different, disjointed and, I suspect, far less fulfilling experience for all of us.

Peter Boardman, Chris Bonington, Al Rouse and Joe Tasker reached the summit of Kongur on 12th July 1981. Scarcely had they returned to Base Camp than my own thoughts turned to the following year. The Kongur equipment, all well travelled and battered, needed reorganising. I had the unusual task of packing the main supplies for Everest in Western Xinjiang in the few days' rest we had at Kongur Base Camp before returning home. A complex baggage manifesto, varying from scientific equipment bound for Britain, tents for Hong Kong, oxygen cylinders to await our return in Peking, was typed in quadruplicate at Base Camp, boxes checked, sealed and finally abandoned in Kashgar. 'Don't worry,' our liaison officer, Mr Liu Dayi, announced, 'if it is labelled correctly there is no problem.' It was true. It is a tribute, indeed, to the Chinese that our only permanent losses in three years of expeditions through the People's Republic and Hong Kong occurred in London at Heathrow Airport, a sad reflection on the capitalist world.

The Kongur Expedition returned to Britain on a sunny morning early in August 1981. I realised with a surging sense of panic that there were to be but six months in Britain before we were off again. There was much to do. Chris immersed himself in the Kongur book with his usual dedication, dividing time sparingly between his life as author, lecturer and Everest leader.

Whilst many of the details of our plans for Everest were similar to Kongur, the form of the expedition was to be very different. Our team was to be six instead of ten and the whole emphasis was to be on as small, self-sufficient, and light a scale as the objective would allow us. The climbing team was to be four in number, supported by two 'low-altitude staff' of which I was to be one.

Chris is now forty-eight, one of the most experienced high-altitude mountaineers. Expeditions have been his life since 1960, following at almost annual intervals, notably the first great face climb of an 8000-metre peak, Annapurna South Face in 1970, his attempt on Everest's South West Face in the autumn of 1972, its successful ascent in 1975, Brammah in 1973, Changabang in 1974, the Ogre in 1977. I had known Chris well since Everest in 1975. I had been impressed both with his power as a leader, which he liked to exercise from as near the vanguard of an expedition as possible, and by the meticulous attention he paid to detail. In contrast Chris's ability to change his mind about major decisions is perhaps a source of amusement to those who know him well. At its best it reflects the unusual quality of being able to listen to advice and it ensures that those who know him don't miss expedition meetings by sleeping late.

Coupled with his undoubted abilities there are sides to Chris's intimate life that few of us envy and even fewer wish to share. He is a deep-sleeper whose snores can be heard from a great distance and have once been mistaken for the approach of wolves, and an execrable chef whose nadir of culinary achievement was to ruin an entire and most precious meal high on Kongur by mistaking lemonade powder for potato powder.

Peter Boardman was a relative newcomer to the Himalayan scene when I met him on Everest in 1975. He had then been twenty-four. His outstanding performance there was to make the second ascent of the South West Face with Sherpa Pertemba. It was Peter who had waited in vain on the South Summit of Everest in appalling weather for Mick Burke to return, struggling back to Camp 6 in a storm which marked the closing stages of the South West Face Expedition. He had been pushed to fame and followed Everest with a succession of extraordinary high-altitude climbs, typified by bold routes on great mountains with minute expeditions, several shared with Joe Tasker.

I had known Peter for seven years and had seen him emerge into maturity. I learnt that beneath what was at first sight a veneer of relaxation was an almost superhuman driving force, spurring on each expedition. On a trip Peter was a tidy, clean, organised man who valued his solitude and during long hours alone would write profusely and study his subject in depth. On Kongur and on Everest he was the natural mountain historian, collecting information in an ordered and interesting way. His concentration on writing had already borne fruit. His first book, *The Shining Mountain*, an account of climbing the West Wall of Changabang with Joe Tasker, had won the John Llewelyn Rhys Memorial Prize. While he attempted the North East Ridge of Everest the proofs of his next book, *Sacred Summits*, the story of his remarkable climbs in 1979, were already with his publishers.

If Chris Bonington was to be the example of the public persona on this expedition, Dick Renshaw would be the gentle recluse, ultimately disciplined, dedicated wholly to mountaineering. He had established a particularly strong climbing partnership with Joe Tasker, who wrote of him, 'In smoking, as in all things, Dick was completely controlled. He would take along one cigarette for each bivouac, so friends could estimate how long he thought a climb might take by the number of cigarettes. Three meant a serious route.' Dick had proved himself as a mountaineer with major contributions to make, first by his winter ascent of the Eiger with Joe in 1975 and later that year in their extraordinary two-man ascent of Dunagiri, 7066 metres, in the Garhwal Himalaya. This was one of the first difficult routes attempted by a two-man team and with similar ventures of others pioneered a new era of high-altitude mountaineering – small expeditions climbing Alpine-style.

While Dick survived Dunagiri he was not unscathed: exhausted near the summit, he had lost his gloves in the descent and his hands were severely frostbitten. My introduction was a telephone call to the Middlesex Hospital in 1975. 'Hello, I'm Dick Renshaw. A surgeon at home wants to amputate my fingers and says I'll never climb again. Do you agree?' We saw a lot of each other during the treatment for his frostbite and he managed to avoid all but trivial amputation. He has certainly climbed again.

The fourth of the climbing team was to be Joe Tasker. His climbing life was inextricably linked, first with Dick, on the Eiger and on Dunagiri, and later with Pete on Changabang and Kangchenjunga. He had also been to K2 with Chris and Peter in 1978, an expedition which had been abandoned after the death of Nick Estcourt. He attempted the West Ridge of Everest in the bitter cold of winter in 1979 but returned, undeterred, to try K2 with Peter, Dick and Doug Scott in 1980. This expedition, too, had failed as they were all but swept from the mountain by avalanches. Success on Kongur followed in 1981. Spare, with a halo of thinning, dishevelled hair, Joe had a reputation for argument, a brittle veneer that vanished quickly as I grew to know him – usually on excited evenings in our house as he left for the Himalaya.

With the wealth of expedition experience, Joe, too, turned to writing. I wondered sometimes if he felt upstaged by the success of Peter's *The Shining Mountain*. If so, there was no need. In 1981 he was correcting the proofs of *Everest the Cruel Way* as we flew to China and he followed this with a moving climbing autobiography, *Savage Arena*. Joe's second creative talent was in photography and filming. With characteristic enthusiasm and order he had, in 1981, learnt the skills necessary for high-altitude filming and throughout this trip to Everest thought, shot and lived the film he was never to see.

Adrian Gordon, thirty-five, was to be my companion on the lower slopes of Everest. Being an executive of the Royal Hong Kong Jockey Club is an unlikely background for a member of a major Himalayan expedition, suggesting either a bookmaker or an expert trainer. Adrian loves neither gambling nor horses but has a passion for the Far East. From a military family, he served in the Seventh Gurkha Rifles both in Nepal and Hong Kong before leaving in 1972 to work for peaceful ends with the Gurkha Re-integration Scheme in Nepal. We had met in 1975 in Nepal when with his fluent Nepali he had organised Sherpas, camps and equipment on the South West Face. Like myself he had few aspirations to go high but knew that expeditions require organisers as well as a summit team. It was Adrian's thankless task to sort out our grubby gear from Kongur, mend tents, check equipment as it arrived either by sea from China or by air from Britain, and organise much of the food and camping equipment in Hong Kong.

I regarded my own selection as something I did not wholly deserve. Though I had already made several modest Himalayan climbing trips, the 1975 Everest South West Face Expedition taught me for the first time the flavour of a large expedition, its tensions, the meaning of total commitment, the joy of success and the pain of death. I learnt by attrition of the fears and failings of some great climbers and gained useful knowledge of illness at high altitude. For six years I longed to return, particularly to Central Asia. My medical career did not seem to suffer from my previous absences, indeed they may have helped it, and having to my surprise been appointed as a neurologist at St Bartholomew's Hospital in London in 1979, I found support from my colleagues when I planned to visit Kongur in 1981. Once again I failed to distinguish myself as a climber, being unwell above 5500 metres and having a close brush with a windslab avalanche on an easy peak near Base Camp. I thought frequently that three months in Tibet would be too much for me and waited to be told by the others that a stronger replacement would be necessary. As it turned out, nobody seemed worried about my failures and when we returned to London in August 1981 I found myself once again immersed in food lists, medical supplies and organisation for Everest.

This then was our team; a party of six very different people all related by a common cause and unanimous in the goal we had set ourselves. We seemed, for Everest, to have one great asset. Almost all of us knew each other well, trusted each other implicitly and were intent upon success. Neither bravado, internal jealousy nor over-confidence were components in the family atmosphere of this expedition. We were not without argument but we were free of the seeds of bitterness. It seemed to me that at least we would enjoy ourselves in Tibet.

I often feel that the preparations for an expedition are like the description of a first pregnancy – of intense interest and importance to the participants but certainly not unique. While Adrian packed in Hong Kong, Chris, Pete and Joe organised the high-altitude equipment in Britain; Dick and I looked after the food. There were no committee meetings. We packed early in January during a weekend when Britain was paralysed under a layer of ice and snow. Somehow we all reached Manchester and I slept on crates outside the Jardines' warehouse, snug in several sleeping bags with the temperature at – 12°C.

There was a sombre undercurrent, an element of finality as we packed our belongings – most of which we would next see in the Rongbuk Valley of Tibet. For Joe, Pete, Chris and Dick there would be high risks near the summit of Everest. I wondered how they felt, that icy weekend. For myself awareness of the dangers of high-altitude mountaineering is never far from the surface. I had seen death on one expedition and had lost friends on others. So had we all. It is well known that a fatal accident occurs more often than not on expeditions over 8000 metres. Together we felt we shared the responsibility for the task we had chosen to undertake. Fear colours my own climbing and has made me gradually less ambitious, content with modest climbs and to expand my interest in high-altitude medicine rather than pursue ever-increasingly challenging objectives.

In Manchester we read the Bonington masterplan, fresh from his Wang word processor.

1st March   *Depart London Heathrow, Flight No.* BA003
2nd March   *Arrive Hong Kong*
7th March   *Fly Chengdu – Lhasa, Flight No.* CA4403
16th March *Arrive Everest Base Camp with Jardines' trekking team*
Mid-May   *Attempt summit*

It all had a familiar ring – we would be leaving in six weeks.

2: Goddess Mother of the World

1st–8th March/Charles Clarke

Parting becomes harder each time we go. A strange distance begins to build up the week before with each decision about my patients, house, friends and family having an uncanny finality. I shop at Sainsbury's for the last time, bringing home food that I won't be eating. I clean the drains and pay the telephone bill. Ruth, my wife, finds it hard and does not hide her feelings. 'I wish you were gone and have done so for months; for when you've gone I can at least look forward to the time of your return getting shorter.' My two daughters have their own defences. Total immersion or separation. Ruth keeps apart, as if expedition affairs are part of a religion she wishes to forget. Wendy Bonington keeps apart, too, looks forward to making pots and painting, isolated in her Cumbrian cottage.

Hilary Boardman is different; a climber herself and no stranger to the Himalaya. When we were on Kongur last year she was in India some 300 miles away, climbing new peaks and before, on a pre-marital honeymoon of magic, she had with Peter tramped with the pygmies, clad only in their spectacular penis gourds, through the rain and steam of New Guinea to climb the Carstenz Pyramid. Hilary is involved, part of the fabric of knowledge of our routes, maps, equipment, almost to the extent of being a member of the team. I sometimes feel she is cross she isn't coming with us.

Joe's Maria, slim, fine and rather fierce, has become a part of the outfit too. She knows more of Joe's inner thoughts than anyone else, but not everything for there's always a private side to Joe.

Dick's family I know less well. Jan seems maternal, friendly and quietly resigned to our departure while Daniel, the twenty-month blond image of Dick, potters about in his nappies, chuckling like his dad.

Frenda Gordon is in Hong Kong, their second baby due during the expedition. I dare not think what she will have to go through, all alone while we're away. But she seems to have accepted it readily and doesn't, I believe, realise that expeditions are dangerous. Of course, they shouldn't be for Adrian and me, I repeat to myself constantly, but know that there will be times when I shall be very, very frightened.

The days drag on. A week to go till Monday, 1st March. There are important things to do. The oxygen sets from the States are delayed. Are we really going on an Everest expedition *again* without checking the system, even if we hope not to use it? We had so many oxygen failures on the South West Face in 1975 that more might have cost us the summit. It is extraordinary that there is still no good, light, high-altitude oxygen set. We can send man to the moon . . . but there's no demand for ten sets a year for the Himalaya. Everything comes separately from different firms. From the USA masks from Scott Sierra, regulators from Robertshaw, helmets from Protection Incorporated, adaptors from Rowe Engineering in Islington, bottles from Life Support Engineering in Sussex. Will they all fit together? With the inevitability of Sod's Law, they do not. Friday evening and we leave on Monday. They're not too good at this sort of thing in Tibet, either. Eventually a raid on the anaesthetics laboratory at Barts sorted out the couplings and we had, it seemed, 'a system', yet untested as the oxygen bottles were already in Lhasa. I felt guilty and hoped the boys wouldn't find out.

The weekend was like the closing scenes of a play you hope will end. It was cold and clear in London. I ran on Hampstead Heath on Saturday, a crisp, glittering morning with London stretching out below, its skyline cut out of cardboard, stark in a morning free of haze. An attractive Hampstead-looking couple with Old English sheepdog stroll by, fashionably clad in sheepskin and high boots. I looked at them with a mixture of envy, lust and faint disdain, thinking that they'll be walking their dog next Saturday while I shall be far away, probably in Lhasa.

By Sunday the clan is gathering. Joe telephones to complain bitterly that I have given over our spare double bed to Dick and Jan. Half mocking, 'You know who your real friends are,' he says, 'I expect I'll see you on the 'plane, if you've kept me a seat.' But within a couple of hours Maria and he are around with beer and wine and laughter. Pete flies in from Geneva, alone. Dick, Jan and little Dan. The booze flows as we have a faintly strained evening, torn between two closely cherished loves. One is a wayward mistress, seductive beyond belief. We all want to get moving, to cut the bonds that tie us to work, telephones and responsibility and come to Tibet, to Lhasa, to the mysteries of the northern side of Everest and the North East Ridge. The other mistress is more constant, homely, warmer and reliant. Home, Ruth and two young girls who I put to bed. Rebecca, nine, blonde and thoughtful, insists I promise I shall not venture above Base Camp and volunteers in turn to work hard at school. Naomi, tousled, dark, rowdy and five, simply demands a present from Hong Kong. They scream for Joe to come and kiss them.

We all drank too much to allay our anxieties, turned in too late and woke too early in the tense over-organised fervour of last-minute packing, trying to fight clear of a hangover. The black Jardines' limousines arrived on time and we climbed aboard, watching a silent group on my doorstep. The strain of parting would soon be over and we'd all feel better for it.

Chris keeps somewhat apart on these occasions. He'd stayed the night before 'at his military club in town', which though it sounds like an abode of Biggles in the 'thirties is no more than a sensibly priced and friendly hotel.

It is Chris who has masterminded the publicity of the expedition, helped design a brochure and inform the press. Some climbing purists shun this sort of thing, but we all felt a certain need to explain our aims to the press. Climbing by foreign expeditions is still a very new phenomenon in China and it allows small groups of individuals to penetrate hitherto forbidden areas of the People's Republic – southern Tibet, Xinjiang and remote areas of Sichuan. We were thus in a position of privilege within China, freer than any usual tourist in Tibet. In a genuine, though minor, way our relations with our Han Chinese staff and the local people were also important and could further future co-operation between two countries with histories and aspirations so disparate.

Jardines, our sponsors, were a further reason for the expedition being known. With 150 years of trading and negotiating in China, and a large stake in the economic stability and prosperity of Hong Kong, we wanted to establish in Britain, Jardines' role as sponsors of two major expeditions to China – to Kongur in 1980–81 and to Everest in 1982. Lastly we felt a small part of climbing history, the first expedition from China to Tibet, following the steps of the 1921 Everest Reconnaissance and seven subsequent expeditions. But more than to fulfil a role in an Everest chapter of some encyclopaedia, we wished to see for ourselves a country and a mountain range which had held itself apart, almost untouched for forty years.

For Peter, Chris, Joe and me aboard the British Airways 747 for Hong Kong it was just seven months since we had returned from Kongur – it seemed a little unreal to be going back so soon. I felt poorly informed about the details of the northern approaches to Everest, having had little time to do more than collect the books.

Today there is a vast Everest literature and we had with us many of the major volumes. I settled down like a schoolboy revising for exams to glean the essential information about the northern side. I was soon reading *Mount Everest, the Reconnaissance, 1921*, Sir Francis Younghusband's *The Epic of Mount Everest* and a delightful lighthearted book of Bill Tilman's 1938 Everest Expedition – small like our own.

Everest is, to our generation of climbers, a mountain viewed largely from the south, seen through the haze of the plains of India or from Tiger Hill above Darjeeling. The imperial Survey of India who, under Sir Andrew Waugh, computed in 1852 that Peak XV was, at a little over 29,000 feet (8848 metres), the highest mountain in the world, viewed the mountain from the Nepalese foothills in India. Waugh named the peak after his mentor and previous Surveyor-General, Sir George Everest – a fine example of the authority of the Raj which renamed a peak on the border of two foreign countries, Tibet and Nepal, with a name from village England, quite disregarding its various native names, the most familiar of which was Chomolungma.

To the Tibetan villager, travelling with his yak to new pastures below the Rongbuk foothills, to the Khamba brigand, hiding from pursuing bands of a local warrior lord, or the illegal surveyor from India disguised as a monk, the North Face of Everest would, however, be but one of a group of great peaks in the dry high-altitude rolling plateau of southern Tibet. Even today the traveller might fail to identify the world's highest mountain from the north, until he is well into the Rongbuk Valley.

Perhaps the earliest photographs of Everest from the north were taken from Khamba Dzong, some ninety miles away, by J. C. White, a member of the British Mission to Lhasa led by Colonel Younghusband in 1904. Later in this expedition Major Ryder and Captain Rawling saw the mountain from some sixty miles due north and thought it might be approached from that direction.

Although the Mission to Lhasa established a British presence in Tibet, the xenophobic, monastic oligarchy which ruled the country did not warm to the idea of an expedition to Chomolungma, the Goddess Mother of the World. It was not until 1921, after a successful application by the Viceroy, Lord Chelmsford, had been presented in Lhasa by the British Resident of Sikkim, Sir Charles Bell, that the first Everest Reconnaissance was permitted, led by Lieutenant Colonel Charles Howard-Bury, an Indian Army officer with a passion for Tibetan exploration, and in particular Mount Everest. He was a tenacious, if opinionated, organiser. Harold Raeburn was climbing leader with George Leigh Mallory, G. H. Bullock and Dr A. M. Kellas, a veteran Himalayan explorer. Majors H. T. Morshead and E. O. Wheeler of the Survey of India, Dr A. M. Heron of the Geological Survey and Dr A. F. R. Wollaston, explorer, naturalist and physician, completed the party.

The achievements of the Reconnaissance were considerable for they explored, mapped and climbed around several thousand square miles of unknown ranges and glaciers on the northern and eastern sides of Everest. Travelling largely on horseback, they first crossed the Himalaya from Darjeeling and travelled west along the southern fringe of the Tibetan plateau. Illness struck early on the trip and Dr Kellas died, it was thought of pneumonia, shortly before reaching Khamba Dzong – thus depriving the team of the most experienced Himalayan mountaineer of the day. Raeburn also fell ill and played little part in the expedition thereafter.

The northern approaches to the mountain were first explored, the West and Central Rongbuk Glaciers. They confirmed the impression from distant views that Everest was a huge pyramidal peak of three great ridges and three faces. The West Ridge and North Face were felt to be out of the question for a first ascent. The upper reaches of the long North East Ridge above 8400 metres did, however, look feasible and from the northern side of the mountain it was clear that a straightforward secondary ridge joined this arête, leading from a col at 6990 metres to the crest at about 8230 metres. The western approaches to this col (the North Col or Chang La) looked hazardous and the climbing party, comprising by this time only of Mallory and Bullock, believed that the only way to explore the eastern side of the North Col was to travel north around Everest to the Kharta and Karma valleys, which they assumed would in some way lead to the North Col. Having travelled to Kharta by the Doya La they crossed a 5300-metre pass, the Langma La, to Karma, a broad fertile valley with a spectacular southern wall formed by the precipices of Chomo Lonzo, Pethangtse and Makalu. Filling the head of the Karma Valley was the huge Kangshung Face of Everest, framed to the south by the South Col, 7986 metres, and South East Ridge, and to the north by the long North East Ridge and the Raphu La, 6510 metres. Neither looked a feasible proposition. The eastern side of the North Col was still elusive, although the expedition survey party had outlined a route there from the Rongbuk Valley via the East Rongbuk Glacier. The team ended their stay in the autumn of 1921 by travelling up the Kharta Valley over the Lhakpa La, a pass at 6705 metres. From there Mallory, Bullock and Wheeler, accompanied by their porters, descended to the head of the East Rongbuk Glacier and made a spirited climb to the North Col of Everest. Above lay the buttresses of the North Ridge which looked reasonable ground for a future attempt on the mountain.

In three months of intense activity the Tibetan side of Everest had been explored. Only the Western Cwm and the South West Face remained as unknown pieces of the jigsaw but these lay in the forbidden land of Nepal – and would be, in any case, extremely difficult of access from Tibet by either the South Col or the Lho La. Mountaineers were to wait some thirty years before approaching the massif from the south. The mountaineering achievements of reaching the North Col and climbing several 6000–7000-metre peaks were considerable and the detailed surveys of Morshead and Wheeler were to form the basis of all maps of the Everest region. Heron had carried out a geological survey (much to the distaste of the Tibetans who thought he would disturb the deities of the rocks with his hammer) and Wollaston had made a valuable record of the flora and fauna of the region.

The composition and prejudices of the 1921 Reconnaissance were those which would mark many succeeding expeditions to Everest. The team was chosen not by the leader but by the Everest Committee, joint child of the Royal Geographical Society and the Alpine Club, who naturally chose gentlemen who were army officers or graduates of the older universities. The press at first were rigorously excluded by A. R. Hinks, Secretary of the Royal Geographical Society, although under pressure he relented. His attitude is summed up in a letter to Howard-Bury during the expedition. 'We don't know the way about among all these sharks and pirates . . . we are having a devil of a time over these sharks who want photographs. No-one regrets more sincerely than I do that any dealings with the press were ever instituted at all.'

An aloofness seems to have pervaded the Reconnaissance, exemplified in the closing chapter of the 1921 book. Here Norman Collie, the President of the Alpine Club, wrote his appreciation in which he omitted to mention at all four members of the team – Raeburn, the climbing leader, Wollaston, a notable explorer and naturalist, Heron the geologist, and poor Dr Kellas who lost his life.

Most of the expedition members had at least one personal target of detestation. For Mallory it was Howard-Bury and Raeburn, both of whom he found irritating. The team's action seemed to exemplify this lack of harmony with Mallory and Bullock's failure to find the East Rongbuk Valley which can only be regarded as an error of major proportions – forcing the expedition to march nearly a hundred miles to its new Base Camp at Kharta. Surely a team with a specialist, highly experienced survey party (Wheeler was later to become Surveyor General of India), should use it to liaise with the climbing team in finding a route to the mountain, rather than leave it to work as a separate unit?

For life at high altitude there seems to have been little overt preparation. Although Trisul (7120 metres) had been climbed in 1907 and many of the effects of lack of oxygen and cold documented on previous expeditions to the Himalaya and Andes, there seems to have been little rigorous emphasis on acclimatisation. The choice of equipment was even left to individuals, an allowance of £50 being made for each man to buy his own boots and clothing.

The 1922 expedition led by Brigadier-General Bruce was a team of thirteen Britons who followed the East Rongbuk Glacier route and camped on the North Col on 18th May – the first time man had camped above 6900 metres. On 27th May George Finch (the father of the actor, Peter) and Captain Geoffrey Bruce (the General's nephew) reached 8320 metres, using oxygen – the first time that it had ever been used on a climb. On a subsequent assault on 7th June seven porters were killed in an avalanche en route to the North Col, an indication of how dangerous these slopes could be after fresh snowfalls. General Bruce recorded his interpretation of the Tibetan reaction tersely in his account of the expedition. 'If it was written that they should die on Everest, they should die on Everest; if it was written that they would not die on Everest, they would not, and that was all there was to be said in the matter.' Despite this accident, plans were soon afoot for the 1924 expedition.

It was on this famous assault, again led by General Bruce (though he had to retreat with malaria on the march in), that Norton reached 8550 metres without oxygen. This was followed by Everest's most famous tragedy, the loss of George Leigh Mallory and Andrew Irvine. They were last seen near the crest of the North East Ridge, above the North East Shoulder, at a height greater than 8500 metres. Their bodies were never recovered, though an ice axe belonging to the pair was discovered later. Two other deaths took place on this expedition, almost forgotten in the drama of the loss of the favourite sons of England – Lance-Naik Shamsherpun died following a stroke and assistant boot-maker Bahadur died of pneumonia following frostbite. Their names were recorded on a memorial cairn with those of the dead of 1921 and 1922.

Political troubles, caused in part it is thought by the behaviour of the 1920s parties (shooting wildlife, collecting geological specimens and travelling to unspecified areas) and in part by the loss of life (Everest expeditions had already claimed twelve lives), prevented further visits to Tibet for nine years. British expeditions again tried Everest by the North Col route in 1933, 1935, 1936 and 1938 but each, usually because of bad weather, turned back below the 8550-metre record set by Norton in 1924. Such failures served only to increase the mystique of this, the highest mountain.

Two other events in Everest's history before the second world war should not be forgotten. In 1933, still in the period when the history of aviation was fired by personal ingenuity and courage, sometimes to the point of lunacy, two aircraft flew over the summit of Everest. It was not the first time the idea of flying to Everest had been mooted, for Howard-Bury had visited the air force in India in 1920. Initially he was given a cold shoulder, though later enthusiasm seems to have been rejected by the Everest Committee on the grounds of finance. The Houston Everest flight on 3rd April 1933 was carried out in two Westland aircraft powered by the new supercharged Pegasus S3 engines. The Everest flight deserves to be remembered, not for its achievement as a high-altitude stunt, but as an expedition which was organised with exemplary efficiency. Oxygen equipment, cameras and clothing were all heated by ingenious low-voltage systems (modified for the specific purpose) and great attention given to the preparation of weather reports from Calcutta and from the expedition's own high-altitude balloon.

Another prewar visit to Everest had a less happy ending. Maurice Wilson, an eccentric Yorkshireman with almost no climbing or flying experience, decided to pilot himself to Everest and climb the mountain solo, relying on a diet of rice and spiritual determination achieved by meditation. Despite every step of his journey being forbidden or frustrated by the British government or the government of India, he eventually flew to India, smuggled himself to Tibet in 1934, and died, presumably of hypothermia, below the North Col. His body was discovered by Charles Warren, doctor and climber on the 1935 expedition, led by Eric Shipton.

In the decade following the second world war Everest's Tibetan side received little attention, when Nepal, previously a country even more secretive than Tibet, began to open its borders. A little was known of the southern side, for Mallory had seen it from the West Rongbuk Glacier in 1921 and before, in 1907, Nata Singh, of the Survey of India had visited the Dudh Kosi Valley and mapped the snout of the Khumbu Glacier. In the summer of 1950 an Anglo-American reconnaissance expedition reached the Khumbu Glacier from Nepal, and was followed next year by a British and New Zealand team led by Eric Shipton. The first and second attempts on the mountain by the South East Ridge by the Swiss expeditions of 1952 were unsuccessful. The following year the summit was reached via the South

East Ridge by the Sherpa Tenzing Norgay and the New Zealander, Edmund Hillary, members of the British expedition led by John Hunt. The southern side of Everest has had, since then, almost annual visits and the original route has been climbed by nineteen expeditions, with ascents by ninety-one individuals to date.[1] The other frontier ridge – the West – was climbed by the Americans in 1963 by a route that included several hundred metres on the North Face – and later by the Yugoslavs in 1979. The South West Face of Everest, rising out of the Western Cwm, was climbed in 1975 after five previous attempts. On this expedition, led by Chris Bonington, Dougal Haston, Doug Scott, Peter Boardman and our Sirdar Pertemba, reached the summit. Adrian Gordon and I had been part of the support team. Our success had been marred by the tragedy of losing Mick Burke, climber and cine photographer, who was last seen heading upwards, a few hundred metres below the summit. The South Buttress of the South West Face was later climbed by a Polish expedition in 1980.

In contrast the Tibetan faces and ridges of Everest seem almost to have been forgotten in the fervour of the 'fifties, 'sixties and 'seventies, the 'Golden Age' of mountaineering in Nepal. Several parties made illegal visits to the Tibetan side; in 1947 Earl Denman, Canadian by birth and by account a loner with little mountaineering experience, travelled through India to Tibet, reaching a point below the North Col with his Sherpas, Tenzing Norgay and Ang Dawa, both so famous in later years. Again in 1951 another clandestine trip to Everest and Tibet was made by a Dane, Klaus Becker-Larsen, who travelled illegally through Nepal to Khumbu. He first attempted the dangerous Nepalese face of the Lho La (6006 metres) and narrowly escaped being hit by rockfall. Later, with four Sherpas, he crossed the Nangpa La (5716 metres) into Tibet and, like Denman, made his way by the Rongbuk Valley to the East Rongbuk Glacier. Again this ill-conceived attempt failed below the North Col and Larsen returned, alive but undetected by the Chinese, to Namche Bazar.

A further sortie into Tibet from Nepal took place in 1962. An American expedition of four, led by Woodrow Wilson Sayre, grandson of the former President, set out with Sherpas and a liaison officer, ostensibly for Gyachung Kang (7922 metres), a neighbour of Everest. Their aim was to climb a huge icefall below the Nup La, cross this 5985-metre pass and descend to the Rongbuk Glaciers. In a sense this small team was brilliantly successful, proving that a team unsupported by Sherpas can travel and be self-sufficient over long distances at high altitude. After a series of attempts they reached the North Col and finally abandoned the expedition at about 7600 metres. They were lucky to return to Nepal alive and undiscovered by the Chinese. The sequel to this illegal journey, and several other flagrant violations of 'the rules', led to the Nepal Himalaya being closed to expeditions from 1964 to 1969 – a reminder of how mountaineering can depend upon the fickle whim of governments.

*

[1] March 1983.

I had hoped to read of the Chinese' own expeditions to Everest before we touched down at Hong Kong on the morning of 2nd March. We were, as ever, made to feel VIPs by Jardines as we were ushered through the airport into several waiting Mercedes. Little was new here for most of us, from the chauffeurs who knew us by name and the immaculate Jardines offices in the Connaught Centre, to the measured luxury of the Excelsior Hotel. Friends from the previous year greeted us and with bearded smile Adrian Gordon told us soon after our arrival that Frenda had had their baby, another son, and all was well.

A typed programme was in our room; there would be little time to think about jet lag after a twenty-hour flight. Within two hours we were reporting for duty at the helicopter pad of HMS *Tamar* for a flight around Hong Kong. Skyscrapers flashed by, ships in the harbour grew small like toys in a game – 'You know what separates the men from the boys? The size of their toys.' We had left the commercial centre and were skimming green hills, thinly wooded slopes running to remote beaches, out towards the New Territories, and the Chinese mainland. Here, at the eastern end of the frontier, is the town of Lo Wu, pierced by the railway and road to the People's Republic. From the air Lo Wu exposes an uneasy contrast between the People's Republic and the colony of Hong Kong not, on the face of it, flattering to Hong Kong. To the northern side are the grey and white blocks of an ordered town with empty streets, bicycles and few vehicles; this is the People's Republic. Yards away in Hong Kong there is a bustling mixture of apartment blocks, offices, bazaars and a sprawling shanty town seething with people, cars, bicycles and carts.

We flew along the deserted land border where a high fence now marks a No Man's Land. Illegal immigration to Hong Kong has, to a large extent, been curbed by increased Chinese vigilance and constant patrols by land, sea and air from Hong Kong. We saw no fugitives but the previous year Peter told me that he had seen two corpses huddled, half-sunk in the mud flats near the border.

The pace of these two days was hectic. A serious beer session with our pilots was followed by a ceiling writing competition. Joe won with an unlikely poise from his belt slung over the girder above the bar. Dinner in the mess with Gurkha stewards, chicken and chips and too much wine. I fell asleep in the car on the way home to the hotel and awoke, over-excited but ready for more, the night ending in an excess of alcohol for us all in the hotel. Perhaps wiser than the rest of us, Chris slipped off to bed, he usually does.

Chris and I had one more day in Hong Kong before leaving for Peking. Adrian, Dick, Joe and Peter and the Jardines' trekking party who were coming to Base Camp were to fly to Chengdu, capital of Sichuan Province, where we were all to reunite before flying to Lhasa. March 4th was a hurried day of meeting the Hong Kong press, last minute shopping in the land of plenty, refills for ball pens, diaries, the final additions to the Cannon and

Olympus camera paraphernalia – and more over-excited entertainment far into the small hours.

By noon next day we were in Peking, re-united with more friends from Kongur: David Mathew, a languid Old Etonian, who is the Jardines' Peking Manager, his assistants, Alison Hardy and Peter Po – an emigré from mainland China whose home is now Hong Kong.

Despite being amongst friends, I felt uneasy to be back in China and anxious to leave for Lhasa. What a contrast to the year before when every aspect of Chinese life fascinated me in this Third World nation which is so different from the rest of Asia. Previously I had been impressed with the order, health, civility and efficiency. Here was Peking, a city with streets cleaner than London, free of beggars and where appointments are on time. It was, however, now the drabness which overwhelmed me. Peking seemed a grey city, all the greyer in March before the green of spring, sprawling without form around the vastness of its central Tian-an-men Square.

We were not in Peking to see the sights, but to put together the pieces of the bureaucratic jigsaw which are an integral part of any expedition to China. The Chinese Mountaineering Association, with headquarters in Peking, is an organisation which includes amongst its functions the super-vision of the day-to-day management of all foreign expeditions.

The meeting with the CMA was, as usual, formal and to the point. We met Mr Shi Zhanchun, the Vice-Chairman, a warm and enthusiastic man who welcomed us back as old friends. Mr Chen Rongchang, who was to be our liaison officer, had had his nose, hands and ear frostbitten on a previous visit to Everest. He was impressively efficient and through our interpreter, Mr Yu Bin, asked us questions about our own plans which we could not answer in the detail required. 'On what date exactly will you require the nine yaks at Base Camp?' Three thousand miles away in a land where neither the British nor most Chinese could speak the language.

Mr Shi has been associated with mountaineering in China since the 1950s and particularly with Everest. He led the first Chinese Everest Expedition in 1960 – a massive affair with over 200 members. Mr Shi himself climbed above 8000 metres and his mountaineering experience is abundantly obvious in conversation. In our meeting with the CMA and at a banquet which followed in the evening, we wanted to piece together a few missing links in the story of Chinese activity on Everest on the Tibetan side.

We still know very little about the early visits of the 1950s. It is widely rumoured that a Russian expedition went to Everest in 1952. A forty-man team, led by Dr Pavel Datschnolian, was believed to have reached 8200 metres before six members were lost, including the leader. Whether or not this report has any foundation will probably never be known: the very existence of the expedition was formally denied in 1974 by the President of the USSR Mountaineering Foundation. Tactful questions to the Chinese – for Sino-Soviet relations are still a subject which may provoke embarrass-ment and hostility – brought the response that Mr Shi was unaware of any

Russian expedition to Everest, although it was agreed that Russia 'helped' in a reconnaissance expedition of 1959.

We shall probably never know all the details of Chinese visits to the mountain, but we seem to have some fairly definite events on which to build a Chinese Chomolungma calendar.

In 1958 the First Chinese Reconnaissance took place, a multi-disciplinary scientific and mountaineering expedition. The Second Reconnaissance followed the next year and the road to and beyond Rongbuk was built. In 1960 the first Chinese Chomolungma Expedition, led by Mr Shi Zhanchun, climbed the mountain by the North Col route. For the first time yaks were used instead of porters to carry loads to Advance Base Camp at 6500 metres.

On this expedition, after a determined first assault by Mr Shi and Wang Feng-Tung, who almost reached the top of the Second Step on the summit ridge at 8600 metres, the mountain was climbed by Wang Fu-Chou, Chu Yin-Hua and Konbu during the night of 24th–25th May. The account of this expedition, whose success was doubted for many years in the Western climbing press, is still hard to follow. This is explained, I believe, by poor translation and a total lack of experience of the expedition's press agents, accompanied by incomplete photographic corroboration. Looking back nearly twenty-five years later and having now met the leader, Mr Shi, and others who were on the trip, I find every reason to applaud the very considerable achievements of the party.

During our visit to Peking we learnt for the first time of a Second Chinese Chomolungma Expedition in 1964 and later checked our interpretation of the facts with Mr Chen, our liaison officer, who had been a team member. This pre-monsoon expedition was the first to set foot on the North East Ridge from the Raphu La and reached about 7000 metres before turning back. There was also an unsuccessful attempt by the North Col route. We were told that this expedition was in preparation for one on a larger scale in 1965 a trip that never took place, probably because of the Cultural Revolution.

Mystery surrounds the events of the next decade. A report in *Alpinismus* in 1967 rumoured that a Chinese expedition had suffered a massive accident the previous year in which twenty-six people had died and there was a suggestion in *Mountain* (No. 8, 1970) that a team of three surveyors had reached the summit, apparently separately, in 1969. My hunch is that these tales are both untrue, but that several small expeditions of scientists and surveyors visited Chomolungma in the late 'sixties and no ascent was made or even intended. For these were troubled times in recent Chinese history with the Cultural Revolution at its height and internal difficulties within Tibet.

The most recent Chinese ascent was in 1975. This expedition was again led by Mr Shi and was a large team accompanied by scientists and a film crew. Nine climbers – seven Tibetan men, one Tibetan woman and one Han Chinese – reached the summit on 27th May 1975, using intermittent oxygen. The ascent was filmed, including the final steps to the summit, by telephoto. Important and unusual scientific work was carried out – for example an electro-cardiogram was recorded on the summit. An aluminium survey pole was left on the top (if doubt remained for outsiders!) and was discovered by Doug Scott and Dougal Haston after the first ascent of the South West Face from Nepal that autumn.

In 1982 ours was the fourth expedition since 1975 on the Chinese side. A joint Sino-Japanese team climbed a new route in the North Face in 1979 and was followed by Reinhold Messner's remarkable solo ascent without oxygen by the North Col route in 1980. A large French military expedition attempted the North Col route in the spring of 1981 but failed because of bad weather, reaching a height of 8200 metres. In the autumn of the same year an American team were the first to attempt the huge Kangshung Face. They succeeded in climbing a steep and very difficult rock buttress at the foot of the face, reaching a height of about 7000 metres before turning back.

This in outline was the sum of our knowledge about the Chinese side of the mountain and I was relieved to discover that there had been no further activity on the long North East Ridge. I had half expected that we would be told gently and in passing that the Chinese climbers went barefoot from the Raphu La to the North East Shoulder on several occasions!

And so on the morning of 6th March, Chris and I left Peking along the long avenue to the airport with Mr Chen, our liaison officer, and Mr Yu, our interpreter. David Mathew, hating air travel as much as I do, would accompany us as far as Xegur, our last town in Tibet. We were off at last for Chengdu, en route for Lhasa.

3: Lhasa, once Forbidden City

8th–16th March/Charles Clarke

A turbo-prop Ilyushin roared into the darkness of a warm, soggy Chengdu dawn; within an hour we were in daylight, not too far above the ground which was a spectacular range of peaks in eastern Tibet, many over 6000 metres high. I was unprepared for both the fierceness and scale of the terrain below us. How different from the Tian-shan range (in Xinjiang) which the previous year had seemed fairly gentle hills, sometimes covered with snow. But these Tibetan peaks stretched as far as the eye could see on either side of the aircraft, for forty-five minutes' flying at 350–400 knots, and were the sharpest range of mountains I had ever seen – viciously sharp, towering ridges with knife edges, fluted ice gutters and spiky summits so thin that it looked as if you could scarcely straddle them. They are, I suppose, 6000–7000 metres high; not one of the major peaks has ever been visited.

We dropped then through lower hills, sandy, barren wastes, and flew along the Tsang Po which, renamed the Brahmaputra, takes an un-scheduled turn south into Assam. The airfield is two hours' drive from the rest house (why, I wondered – because it's easier to defend?), which is just over a mile out of central Lhasa, tucked into a military complex. There were ten field guns next door to us. There, across the valley floor, the Potala Palace loomed in the distance like some vast fortress, its features blunted by haze, rising incongruously out of the modern Lhasa of corrugated roofs and concrete blocks. We came to see the Potala in its true beauty as we drove to town that afternoon. It was saved from appearing dull and monolithic by a subtle tapering in all its dimensions, in every fold of the walls. The result is a vast structure poised lightly on a hill. It is one of the most beautiful buildings I have ever seen.

Our large party was feeling the strain of the altitude at 3600 metres. The climbing team seemed well enough but some of the trekkers looked tired and ill. I felt lethargic, too, barely able to drag myself the 200 metres to the compound's dining room. From now on I had to be vigilant about our health and hoped that in the week to come we could avoid the more unpleasant forms of altitude sickness. We began to get to know the trekking group better and enjoy the company of ten people who were largely from a world of high finance and commerce. David Newbigging, Chairman of Jardines, with his wife Carolyn had been with us in Xinjiang: we were now used to the idea of living with the 'Taipan' whose word almost alone had, it seemed, financed both the Kongur and Everest expeditions. Martin Henderson, who had personally organised much of this Everest trip, and been with us to Kongur Base Camp, was with us again; previously a stranger to climbing, he had absorbed much of its history and jargon, even taking a course at Peter's International School of Mountaineering in Leysin. There was Piers Brooke, an English banker living in New York, and his wife Suzy who writes children's books; Robert Friend from Jardines in Hong Kong, Andrew Russell from Jardines in Manila and Michael Jardine (no relation), a fluent Mandarin speaker who runs the Jardines office in Shanghai. 'The Pygmies', Steven McCormick and David Livermore, two six foot three American conservationists who were having their first glimpse of Asia, completed the party.

Tibet is, and always has been, a land of mystery and despite having been opened by the Chinese government to selected tours, it is still one of the countries least visited by travellers. For each of us this was to be a treasured experience, probably never to be repeated, and each of us would feel the power of this country, smell it, touch it and perhaps just begin to understand it. In European literature Tibet has been a country which has excited two emotions – inquisitive fascination or disgust. Travellers for centuries, and there have only been a handful until recent times, remarked upon the filth, squalor and disease of Lhasa. Certainly many of the early Everesters did not share our fascination with Tibet. Mallory, who loathed the country and the people, wrote: 'A usual and by now welcome sound in each new village is Strutt's [Deputy Leader of the 1922 Expedition] voice, cursing Tibet – this march being far more dreary and repulsive even than the one before, and this village being more filthy than any other.'

Even as recently as 1955 the journalist Alan Winnington, on a remarkable journey through eastern Tibet to Lhasa, wrote of the capital: 'Open heaps of rubbish – which are traditionally cleared once a year – lie along some streets, a mixture of rotting substances from which the purple green carcass of a decomposing dog juts out. Dogs are everywhere . . .'

The two aspects of Tibet which provide much interest to the traveller of the late twentieth century are the incomparable relics of its monastic past and relations between Tibetans and the Han Chinese. Whereas a fable, extolling national virtues and vices, relates that the Tibetan people are descended from the union of a mountain she-devil (deceit, theft and cruelty) and a monkey (wisdom, humanity and piety), the truth of their origins, although more mundane, is far from clear. Nomadic tribes are thought to have settled in Tibet, particularly in the fertile eastern regions, in the first five centuries AD, or possibly earlier. In the seventh century the country was united under a dynasty of warrior kings, Namri and his son, Songsten Gampo (c.627–650AD) who began an era of martial expansion and initiated the relationship with the Chinese throne by marrying Wen Cheng, a princess of the Tang Dynasty. He also married a Nepalese princess and took a Tibetan wife. The Tibetan empire of the seventh and eighth centuries extended far beyond its present frontiers, into Kashmir, Xinjiang, China proper, Bhutan, Sikkim and Nepal; Tibet was a major Central Asian power during this period and dominated the Silk Road through Xinjiang.

The Tibetan empire collapsed in the ninth century and the last Tibetan king was assassinated in about 842. During the internal strife in the three centuries that followed there emerged the religious leaders and the monastic overlords who were to lay the foundations of the country's future theocracy. From the thirteenth to the seventeenth century Tibetan history was influenced by the rise of the Mongols in Central Asia and the country became a vassal state after the Mongol conquest of China at the beginning of this period.

Buddhism, evolving its unique Tibetan form, can be seen as the motive force behind the nation's more recent history. Buddhism became the royal religion with the Chinese princess, Wen Cheng; it replaced but also incorporated much of Bon-Po, a primitive animistic religion which existed in many of the Himalayan countries.

In 1260 Kublai Khan, the Mongol Emperor, invited to Peking, Basba, a prelate of Tibetan Lamaism, leader of the Sakya (Red Hat sect). He is said to have performed many miracles and converted many princes to Buddhism, the Mongolian form of the religion developing thereafter with its headquarters in the holy city of Ulan Bator, the present capital of Outer Mongolia. Basba also created an alphabet for the Mongolian language. In return he was invested with power, both secular and religious, in Tibet which became a part of the Chinese Empire. A century later another powerful prelate, Tsong-kha-pa, initiated a reform movement in an attempt to purge Lamaism of devil worship, corruption and sexual vices. Celibacy was enforced. This reformed sect, the Gelugspa, or Yellow Hats, spread throughout Tibet, monasteries were built, often becoming fortresses, each with a standing army of warrior monks. Rivalry was the rule and in one such period, about 1642, the Gelugspa Head Lama, Ngawang Lobsang, having solicited help from his Mongol overlord, was installed as Dalai Lama – 'The Ocean of Wisdom' – in the Potala Palace in Lhasa. Ngawang Lobsang, the Great Fifth Dalai Lama (the title being conferred retrospectively on his four predecessors), became the religious and secular head of state and succession by reincarnation became a definite doctrine. The office of Panchen Lama, the head of the area around Xigaze, Tibet's second city, was also created about this time.

The inauguration of the Dalai Lamas conferred upon Tibet a monastic dynasty which was to both mould and restrain future development. The monasteries increased in size and wealth, exacting taxes and labour from the peasantry in return for spiritual protection. It was in the interests of the spiritual leaders to eschew all change within Tibet and to resist the influence of foreigners. Lhasa became a Forbidden City, visited by only a handful of travellers until the twentieth century. This policy of isolation, though it created both the unique architectural and artistic splendour of Tibet, paved the way to the country's decline. Because of celibacy the population dwindled. Recorded as 10,000,000–12,000,000 in the twelfth century, it was around 2,000,000 at the Imperial Census of 1795. By the 1953 Chinese census it was 1,000,000 with a further 2,000,000 Tibetans living within Chinese provinces outside Tibet. Meanwhile a poverty-stricken peasant class was maintained on the borderland of slavery by the monks and lay nobles. They were landless, without suffrage, diseased and, it must be surmised, discontented with their lot. Tibet had few relations with foreign countries except China which regarded the Himalayan state as part of its empire. China, under the Manchu Dynasty, occupied Lhasa and in 1788 the Manchu armies were again in Tibet, this time to defend the country against an invasion from Nepal. In the century that followed China maintained its suzerainty over Tibet with varying degrees of strictness, but it was only in 1912 that the Chinese Amban, or Resident, was expelled from Lhasa at the time of the decline and demise of Imperial Peking.

British interest in Tibet increased towards the end of the nineteenth century. There were rumours of Russian influence north of the Himalaya and clandestine visits between St Petersburg and Lhasa, in particular by a mysterious Russian monk named Dorjieff. Prevalsky, the Russian explorer of the nineteenth century, visited the more remote areas of the country, and Britain grew nervous. The British Raj became obsessed with the vision of neutral buffer states to protect the Himalayan frontier of its Indian Empire and determined to establish relations with the Tibetan capital. Having been rebuffed on many occasions, a British force actually invaded Tibet in 1903. Thinly disguised as a political legation, this Mission to Lhasa led by Colonel (later Sir) Francis Younghusband fought several pitched battles, inflicting losses of several thousand on the Tibetan army before it reached Lhasa in 1904, and the Thirteenth Dalai Lama fled to Ulan Bator. This expedition was a large affair, as Peter Fleming records in *Bayonets to Lhasa*:

Animals	Number	Casualties
Mules	7,096	910
Bullocks	5,234	954
Camels	6	6
Buffaloes	138	137
Riding ponies	185	24
Pack ponies	1,372	899
Nepalese yaks	2,953	2,922
Tibetan yaks	1,513	1,192
Ekka ponies	1,111	277

The final entry on the list dealt with two-legged animals:

Coolies	10,091	88

Francis Younghusband, who was later to become a driving force behind the prewar Everest expeditions, had an affection for Tibet but was under no illusion about the inflexible attitudes of the Lamas.

The British, having established a presence in Lhasa, retired to India. Thereafter they had a degree of influence and even started an English school in Gyantse and a permanent British Residence in Lhasa. Relations became more cordial and in the great war Tibet offered support to Britain, an offer politely declined. Until the end of British rule in India in 1947 Tibet remained a remote if civil neighbour north of the Himalaya.

The twenty-five years that followed Indian Independence have been momentous in the history of Tibet. In 1950 the emergent People's Liberation Army, intent on uniting all the former states of Imperial China, invaded eastern Tibet and defeated a Tibetan army at Chamdo. The Fourteenth Dalai Lama fled to India, returning to Lhasa a year later and in September of 1951 the PLA, we are told, 'now entered Lhasa without a shot being fired, with a music band and a concourse of Lamas from the monasteries blowing great silver conches in welcome'.[1] Under the terms of the agreement with China, Tibet was to become a region with local autonomy, freedom of religion and the status and office of the Dalai Lama guaranteed. Changes were, however, to take place which would alter the face and structure of the nation. Roads were built, and a modern communications system set up. Collective farming was introduced and land taken from the monasteries and given to the farming communes. Religion, although not actively suppressed, was not encouraged by the Chinese. Immigration by Han Chinese workers, officials and soldiers took place on a large scale. These changes and the stress imposed upon the old, unflinching monastic order, led to conflict between the Tibetans and Chinese. A revolt in eastern Tibet took place in 1956 and a more widespread but equally unsuccessful uprising in 1959. The Dalai Lama fled to India and, though still the spiritual head of Tibetan Buddhism, lives in exile and has never returned to Lhasa.

But Tibet's troubles were not over, for in 1966 the Cultural Revolution was to cause havoc, bloodshed and destruction throughout the land. Bands of Red Guards, most of whom were young Tibetans, destroyed much of the nation's artistic and architectural heritage which had been preserved by the unchanging order of its clergy and the dry, cold climate. Of over 2000 monasteries and shrines, we were told that under a dozen remain – and we were to see most of them on the journey to Everest.

Passions run high over the rights and wrongs of these unhappy years. Tibet was never, as some suggest, a serene land-locked Himalayan Switzerland and with its heritage and people cared for lovingly by its Lamas. It was a fierce country, cruel and impoverished, held together by the bonds of a religion which, though once a comforter, had become an oppressive force which had sown the seeds of its own demise.

China is today impressively honest about admitting the difficulties it has had with Tibet, although there are dark areas where detail is sketchy. What was apparent during our three months' stay was that Tibet is still nationally remarkably intact, despite the destruction of many of its monuments, and

[1] *Lhasa, the Open City*, Han Suyin. Jonathan Cape, 1977.

there is no attempt on the part of the Chinese to regard the country or the people simply as an extension of the central provinces of the People's Republic. Tibet was, and is, an enigma.

Close to the Potala Palace in central Lhasa is the Jokhang Temple. It is the shrine built to commemorate the coming of Princess Wen Cheng from China in the seventh century and houses the golden Buddha she brought with her. On her arrival at the site of the temple, so the story goes, a spring welled up in response to her presence, beauty and piety. Indeed, in the courtyard there is a well. The Jokhang is encircled by the Parkhor, a bustling array of market stalls, selling shawls, boots, carpets, jewellery and rancid yak butter. Pilgrims mingle in the crowd, walking slowly clockwise round the temple, chanting, 'Om mani padme hum' (Hail to the jewel in the lotus), spinning prayer wheels and plucking rosaries. To gain advancement along the Path of Enlightenment, a few progress by prostrating themselves along the flagstones.

The temple was packed; there must have been about 3000 people inside. The entrance courtyard is black with the grease of prostrating bodies, while a queue, six deep, orderly and mostly silent, wound round the court and disappeared into its inner sanctum. The Jokhang is a place of superlatives and extravagance. In the courtyard were two copper vats some metre and a half across to provide molten rancid yak butter for some 10,000 lights set in rows upon the floor, tended by a few monks. It was once thought that between a quarter and a third of Tibet's butter production went to fuel the lights of its monasteries.

The central hall is about thirty metres square, covered and gloomy, its cloisters supported by pillars fully fifty centimetres square, carved and painted in vivid red and gold. Between the pillars hang thankas, the silk paintings, soiled by grease and smoke but of incredible richness. Thirty-five of these priceless paintings, some said to come from the Tang Dynasty, hang along each of the four walls. From the central roof in swirling smoke, pierced by shafts of sunlight, hang five giant thankas nine metres long and ending high above our heads. Surrounding this hall above the pillars are carved lions, twenty-five to a wall, and signifying either the wrath waiting for the unfaithful or perhaps the might of Imperial China.

Within the hall stands a small shrine filled by the two-metre-high Buddha Princess Wen Cheng brought from China. It is gold, 1200 years old, encrusted with turquoise, coral and other jewels, filling a shrine supported by stone pillars, carved with Tang reliefs. There were other shrines, prayer halls, Buddhas and effigies to monarchs, all rich, dimly lit and filled with the smell of rancid butter smoke, incense, sheepskin and sweat. There was the sound of clashing cymbals, tinkling bells and the low humming prayers of monks and pilgrims.

The Jokhang, packed with people on each day we were in Lhasa, is now clearly a place of fervent prayer, and not at all as described in 1975 by Han Suyin: 'It is obvious that the Jokhang is no longer a place of worship; no crowd is there and except for some incense burning in front of some of the statues, I only noticed one old woman who seemed to be doing some praying.'

From the roof of the Jokhang we peered between the golden domes and spires, looking out on multi-coloured Lhasa. I had never realised that the shutters would be reds and blues, the dresses carmine, purple, green and brown, the high felt boots richly embroidered. The old town surrounds the temple, whitewashed, two-storey houses with painted sills and lintels, each with a frill of cotton fluttering in the breeze. This has changed little, though we saw some fine modern buildings, replicas of old houses recently completed and destined to be dwellings. Above, half a mile away, towers the Potala. The rest of Lhasa is less enticing. Tin roofs and concrete blocks of apartments line the main streets, looking incongruous, ugly and, beside such history, temporary structures.

There is another facet of Tibet's religious past – tolerance. Tucked behind the Parkhor market rises the tiny crescent moon which marks the Lhasa mosque. A bearded old man greeted us with 'Salaam aleikem' and we conducted a halting conversation in smiles and patchy Urdu. The mosque is painted inside in Tibetan style, with Tibetan pictures of Mecca, and adorned by many clocks each telling a different time. Islam has flourished in Tibet for several centuries, apparently untouched by recent troubles. They came, the old man told us, from Kabul. Today a small Moslem community of under a hundred still live, trade and pray in the Lhasa markets.

'Gob smacking, eh?' was Pete's conclusion, covering his literary prowess with language from a childhood in the Scouts. Dick, usually silent, murmured, 'Best sight-seeing I've ever had.' We were all impressed but there was more to come.

Next morning we climbed the steps of the Potala, with Joe filming us. The steps end in a simple entrance some 120 metres above the city. Above it towers the Potala for another 180 metres – it was said to be the tallest building on earth for many centuries. From a distance it may appear to rest lightly upon its hill, but close to it is like standing beneath a mountain rather than a building. For some reason we were not to use the Tibetan entrance at the front but were taken round the back, climbing a steep drive to the back door. Under the old regime nobles on horseback would ride up this hill for a limited distance only, in direct proportion to their rank – while for the common people of Lhasa the palace itself was a Forbidden City. Neither were they permitted even to catch a glimpse of their reincarnate deity, the Dalai Lama. Within the Potala lie the tombs of six Dalai Lamas, and, scattered in a thousand rooms, thousands of little shrines. A morning's visit does little more than convey a general impression of the place; of the thirteen storeys connected by rickety stair ladders; of rows of golden statuettes and of a central shrine, somewhere in the depths of the palace, built as a memorial to King Songsten Gampo and his three wives – Chinese, Nepali and Tibetan. This is the oldest remaining part of the Potala begun in the seventh century. The main structure dates from the seventeenth, when it was rebuilt.

Our visit was conducted through the gloom of dusty passages, half lit by dim electric bulbs. I felt that though the Potala had indeed been lucky to survive the troubles in Tibet, it was no less lucky to have survived its wiring. The electricity system is a maze of exposed cables and frayed insulation all coated with a layer of dust and grease. Some rather hesitant fire extinguishers lurk in the corners, but if the Potala goes up in flames it will be like a torch. I was thinking about the fire risk in a dark corridor when we were suddenly ejected into dazzling sunlight. We were on the roof, perched some 300 metres high above the city, in the courtyard surrounding the Dalai Lama's chambers. 'His palace or his prison?' I wondered, for he had been rarely permitted to leave it.

The last afternoon in Lhasa we spent at the Norbulingka, the Summer Palace, where in shaded, ordered gardens are the summer residences of the previous Dalai Lamas. We saw the Fourteenth's, empty since his departure in 1959. This was a modern Tibet I did not care for. Amid the painted pillars and wall hangings, a broad mirrored staircase swept up to the bedrooms along carpeted corridors. Within the suite there were two Art Deco armchairs, a vast 1940s radiogram with its Garrard turntable upon which rested one HMV 78 rpm record of, of all things, Tibetan Folk Songs. A portable, leather-bound wind-up gramophone lay beside it. Next door a rudimentary bathroom with some fine Shanks 'sanitary ware' – which we were told could not be connected to the plumbing when it arrived – an international, not Tibetan, problem. For me a sense of garish vulgarity pervaded this house and the Summer Palace and I was glad to leave for more earthly pleasures.

Joe, Dick, David Mathew and I, helped by a Tibetan film crew of children, went off to film the Parkhor market. Tourists, though now common enough in Lhasa, are a summer attraction and in March we were the first of the year. Friendly crowds quickly surrounded us, some chanting, others laughing, others trying to sell jewellery, daggers or hats. We were alone for our Chinese staff had, quite wisely, left us to get on with it. We arrived home dusty and exhausted but happy to have had a glimpse of Tibet to ourselves.

We left for Xigaze next morning in the icy dawn of the end of winter. The weather was fine but bitterly cold with night temperatures of $-12°C$. First we crossed the Tsang Po River and drove up to the Khamba La, a 4800-metre pass above the magnificent frozen turquoise lake, Yamdok Tsamdo. We dropped quickly to its shores past a tiny fishing village. Dry hills capped with ice surrounded us. The lake was a haven for migrating wild fowl and quickly the party's ornithologists vied with each other to name nearly twenty species. I tried to join in but, knowing only a few Himalayan birds from previous trips, fell quickly behind Martin Henderson and Andrew Russell – Red Crested Pochard, Mallard, Hen Harrier,

Tibetan Snow Finch, Eurasian Kestrel, Common Pochard, Eurasian Widgeon, Rock Bunting, Little Bunting and Guldenstadt's Redstart. Great Crested Grebe, Ruddy Shellduck, Merganser, Bar-headed Geese, Coots, Hill Pigeon, Dark Kite, Magpie. We drove on, round the lake for some thirty miles, heading for high mountains and climbed a pass of over 5200 metres, the Kharo La. We were following, albeit backwards, the road of the invading British seventy-eight years earlier. The Kharo La has the dubious distinction of marking the site of the highest battle ever fought by British troops: a lonely defile flanked by glaciers where hundreds of Tibetans died for four deaths on the invading side.

We drove on, past Gyantse, scene of another British engagement. This is Tibet's third largest city and perhaps 10,000 people live within it and the surrounding country. We passed by the fine monastery which I visited on a later journey, to be fascinated to see the remodelling of damaged Buddhas being carried out by craftsmen using mud and straw.

We stopped at Xigaze and drove into a compound on the outskirts of the town, the rest house for Chinese officials, drivers, tourists; a friendly place, but faceless. Xigaze is Tibet's second city, the See of the re-incarnate

Panchen Lama. It has one of Tibet's most famous monasteries, the Tashilumpo, founded in 1445. This survives, partially rebuilt. Chris and I slipped out of the rest house next morning and walked over to the monastery. We clambered on to the wall of the Tashilumpo like naughty schoolboys, helped up there by a passing Tibetan, to photograph the golden roofs and the fine long shadows of the early morning. We later paid a more formal visit to the monastery with a Chinese guide who told us that there were now six hundred monks in residence and that children were, once again, being recruited: we saw several boys, their heads shaven, in monks' robes. There were many pilgrims in the courtyard and once again the fervent activity of worship.

Above Xigaze stretches the line of tottering walls of the fort, now in ruins. Martin, the two American 'Pygmies' and I climbed the hill above the town in the afternoon, pleased to be getting some exercise again and relieved that it seemed possible without becoming rapidly exhausted, for we were now at about 4500 metres. The golden roofs of the monastery were far below us, surrounded, as in Lhasa, by an ugly town of modern zinc-roofed buildings.

The road to Xegur, the last town on our journey, was memorable only for its monotony, relieved and enlightened by the Sajia Monastery. Sajia, off the main Xegur–Xigaze highway some 250 miles from Lhasa, was once one of the largest monasteries in Tibet, on the main yak route south. Once there were two monasteries, north and south. Huge and monolithic, it is the southern shrine which survives today. Sajia is an example of ecclesiastical architecture with a military purpose. A castellated square, 200 metres across, flanked by four corner turrets, defends the inner monastery, itself a square of eighty metres. We were conducted inside to an upper dining room with low tables and fine blue and white canvas shutters. After a picnic lunch we entered the inner courtyard through a two-storey portico. Two six-metre-high grotesque figures faced each other across the entrance – a black demon on the left, a red dragon opposite – beckoning us into the main shrine. Inside twenty huge tree trunks (in this treeless land), the largest four fully a metre in diameter, supported the roof and beneath on low carpeted benches was seating for 400 monks. Frescoes stretched from floor to ceiling, nearly twelve metres high, some from the Yuang Dynasty (fourteenth century), but others more obviously Indian and Nepalese. Seven golden Buddhas formed the centrepiece of the shrine, surrounded by hundreds, if not thousands of vases, presents from China long ago. Strangely there were no thankas in this fine hall.

A side hall housed a collection of hundreds of miniatures – Buddhas, statues in gold and a curious plan of the southern monastery housed in a glass case some two metres square. In this the outline of the walls, its entrances and rooms, was etched in powder, made from different coloured salts. There is also a fine library housing several thousand books, mostly printed in blocks on hand-pressed paper, but some were hand written, illuminated with gold on thin slivers of wood. Much of the southern monastery has been finely restored (or possibly never damaged). Not so the northern shrine. David Mathew and I slipped away from our guide, crossed a rickety bridge and climbed quickly into the ruins. Now totally destroyed, a photograph fifty years ago showed that the structure rose in tiers up the hillside, housing 6000 monks. Nothing remains except here and there a patch of wall with the outline of a battered fresco. We were perhaps moved more by this destruction and pillage than by the splendour of the southern buildings.

Xegur Dzong (fort) was still four hours' drive over the dusty rolling highlands. Xegur, which had once been one of the most spectacular dzongs of Central Asia, a military city clinging to a steep hillside, is now a small administrative centre with only the walls of the dzong remaining, etching the skyline in ruined fingers. Tibetans still climb the steps behind it to small shrines, encircling the fort clockwise in a pleasant three-mile hike. We were still acclimatising at around 4000 metres before the final lift to Rongbuk at 5200 metres. We stayed two days, resting, reading, walking or, in the case of Chris, Adrian and myself, lying in bed with the 'flu.

On 16th March we were up before dawn, blow torches trained on the trucks' engines, lighting the barracks with spurts of flame in the bitter cold. The engines, as if to surprise us all, did not explode but burst into life and purred, howled or spluttered through the day. We were off, huddled in duvets, masks and boots, most of us in an open truck, but Joe filming out in front in the jeep. The road to Rongbuk soon left the Friendship Highway from Lhasa/Xigaze/Xegur to Nepal, turned left and headed over a 5000-metre pass. Here we had our first view of the main Himalayan chain, Makalu, Lhotse, Everest, Nuptse, Gyachung Kang and Cho Oyu. We stopped to photograph them all. David Newbigging asked Peter and Chris to identify the peaks and looked a little uncertain as there was disagreement about which was Everest. 'Well, you should know if anyone does.'

We dropped steeply to the valley floor along which the Dzakar Chhu, the river from the Rongbuk Glaciers of Everest, flows eastwards. Soon the river turns south to Kharta on the eastern side of Everest and then cuts through the Himalaya in the gorge of the Arun River, thus delivering all the melt water from the snow and ice of Everest to Nepal. The Dzakar Chhu was beginning to thaw but the ford was iced over, hazardous for trucks. Mr Chen, our liaison officer, had already preceded us and secured, in this unlikely place, a caterpillar tractor which dragged one of our trucks across when it broke through the crust of ice.

We were but a few hours from Everest and the holiday was nearly over, the splendour of a surfeit of monasteries behind us. I felt that these treasures, the glittering jewels luring the sentimental European magpie, had blinded us to another Tibet, a Tibet much harder to reach but more positive. It is difficult to get excited about a tractor, but here was one, not thirty miles from Everest. In two months we would see it ploughing the ground now frozen around us. At Xigaze in the alluvial plain, which is the most fertile land in central Tibet, there are many tractors, ploughs and combine harvesters for the barley – material gains in a country which may have lost its spiritual leadership but also perhaps its former terrible poverty.

The track climbs gently into the Rongbuk Valley, easier and safer than many Himalayan hill roads. It was late afternoon and the weather cloudy as we entered the wide stony floor below the ruined Rongbuk Monastery. Suddenly, it was there, the massive, sombre pyramid of the North Face of Everest, being the only great peak in view, filling the head of the valley ten miles away and 4000 metres above us. True, we had seen photographs, paintings, sketches and even models of the North Face and perhaps we did not have the thrill of Bullock and Mallory's first glimpse in 1921 but here, on a windy afternoon in southern Tibet we were all fulfilling a dream, to visit the northern side of this, the highest mountain. It looked very, very cold.

An hour later, having cut a track through two iced rivers with the help of some local Tibetans (they did it, we watched), and having passed the ruins of Rongbuk, we arrived at a stony plain which was to be our Base Camp at 5200 metres. It was nearly dark, snowing and the wind howled. We had arrived.

4: An icy start

17th March–4th April/Charles Clarke

The first night at Base Camp was a miserable affair. We struggled with the huge mess tent in the wind and snow – we had forgotten how its complex frame of poles clipped together until Martin Henderson, who had solved the problem on Kongur, was summoned to instruct the climbing team. Food was long in coming and meagre when it arrived. There were two events; one which filled us with distaste for fellow mountaineers, the other with anger at our Tibetans. First we realised that we were camping on ground which, though fairly flat, resembled the outskirts of a municipal rubbish dump. Yak dung was acceptable, indeed expected, but not the debris of tins, glass, beer cans, batteries, shreds of clothing, polythene binding, boxes and gas cylinders – their origins all too obvious. 'Principal nocturnal hazard of Base Camp, broken glass.'

Secondly, in unloading the three trucks, we had enlisted the aid of some Tibetan boys who had helped us with the road: within half an hour or so our 220 boxes were in orderly lines but also within that time a remarkable quantity of food and equipment had been slipped deftly into the folds of their clothing. Adrian spotted some losses but first disregarded them – there seemed nowhere the Tibetans could hide much of value. In the end we searched them, each proclaiming his innocence. From a pile of grubby bags and blankets we dug out sweaters, socks, chocolate, film, towels and tins of fruit. The temptation of our array of wealth had been too great and, as if to remind us of their creator, the she-devil of the mountains, they had succumbed. Mr Chen firmly and sensibly told them off but didn't overdo it.

We planned to spend the last two weeks of March acclimatising, staying below 6000 metres, for with a high Base Camp at 5200 metres and easy terrain above, it would have been tempting to rush high too quickly. Even so following a week at around 4000 metres, acclimatisation was being hurried, for after three days at 5200 metres, headaches, lack of appetite and that torpid feeling of exhaustion affected us all. The trekking team were to take part in our high-altitude forays. On 19th March Joe and Pete, with Piers and Suzy Brooke, Robert Friend and Andrew Russell, set off slowly up the Central Rongbuk Glacier to look at the glacial pinnacles below the North Face of Everest. They saw from unusual angles peaks which Joe and Pete knew so well from Nepal – Lingtren, Pumo Ri, Nuptse, Everest's neighbours.

The East Rongbuk team of Chris and Dick, with David Newbigging,

Martin Henderson, Michael Jardine, David Livermore and Steve McCormick, moved up the valley which had seemed so small as to be disregarded by the 1921 Reconnaissance. They placed a camp some three miles away at a point a third of the way between the prewar expeditions' Camps 1 and 2. So we called it Camp 1½ (5650 metres). The next day some of them climbed on to about 5850 metres.

Adrian and I, exhausted after 'flu, and Carolyn, with laryngitis, stayed at Base but it was so cold, even there. Joe had told us all chilling tales of Everest in winter but we never really listened, thinking that by late March and April winter would be behind us and spring – whatever that meant here for there were no flowers or grasses – would be on its way. The first night was below −20°C and by day, though the weather was fine, the temperature was barely above zero with a blustery wind cutting deep into layers of warm clothing.

On 21st and 22nd March the trekkers returned, mostly bearded, grubby and smiling after their trips to high altitude. Joe and Pete carried a load of old tins down from the Central Rongbuk and looked tired. It does one good to remember the stress of early days at altitude where already there is half as much oxygen as at sea level. Everyone looked rotten. Mr Chen was unwell and the cook demoralised by altitude sickness from which I think he never really recovered – the menu for the farewell banquet for the trekkers was not a great success. Next morning we waved goodbye to them and stood, our small team of six, alone with the mountain for the first time.

The plan was simple but we could not carry it out alone: to establish an Advance Base at about 6500 metres on the upper moraines of the East Rongbuk Glacier we needed yaks. We planned to make three ferries which, with the three-day journey up, descent, rest days and bad weather, would take all of a month. Adrian and I were to organise this while the climbers were to push along the North East Ridge. We sat in the mess tent with Mr Chen and our interpreter, Mr Yu, to have the first of many meetings, each of which had an unhurried formality commencing with tea, biscuits and cigarettes. I liked Mr Chen from the start. In his late forties, with a frostbitten face, efficient, quiet, sensible and determined, he was a man whose attitude to our problems, which were legion, was to solve them rather than to ask us to change our minds. Unexpected changes of plan, although part of any expedition, are anathema to the Chinese and it amused me on many occasions to see his look of resigned anguish as he wrote out methodically in a small notebook the third or fourth alteration to a particular phase of the expedition. Mr Chen also knew his ground in the hills: he had been on the mountain twice and had travelled widely in the Everest region. He had earned his position as a committee member of the CMA by long years of hard work.

Mr Yu, a sports interpreter from Peking, was in his early thirties. This was his first visit both to Tibet and to high mountains and his first expedition of any kind, though he had travelled widely with sporting teams to Hong Kong, Pakistan, France and Cuba. His command of colloquial English was excellent and he was prepared to lend a hand with anything – from chipping ice in the frozen river beside camp, loading trucks, cooking, washing up or helping in major administrative decisions.

The Chinese expedition staff were completed by Dawa, a Tibetan truck driver from Lhasa who acted as Tibetan interpreter, and Cheng Wenxin, the jeep driver for whose skill and restraint we were to feel grateful on some of the hill roads. Wang Chouhai, the cook, who seemed unwell and sulky for much of our stay, perked up a little towards the end and produced some reasonable meals.

It is no secret that some foreign climbing teams have had difficulty with their staff and it is important to record that we did not. They worked hard in the monotonous routine of Base Camp life and never hurried us to finish, though it was obvious that they would be glad to get home.

We were not alone for long. Big Lou Whittaker, a giant guide from Seattle, and Jim Wickwire were leading an American team to the North Face. We met them all that evening; fresh faced and friendly, they seemed to have relatively little experience of extreme altitudes. Almost all were guides from Mount Rainier and Marty Hoey, a tall attractive girl, was among them. 'She's just there because she can climb,' drawled one expedition sponsor, Texan Dick Bass. His co-sponsor Frank Wells agreed. Dick and Frank had personally sponsored this American expedition largely to take part in it themselves as a training exercise for a larger project – to climb the highest peak in each continent. With them was a figure from Everest's history, Sherpa Nawang Gombu. He had studied for a year or so in childhood at the Rongbuk Monastery and at the age of seventeen he was on the 1953 Expedition, with the nickname of 'Roly Poly', when he worked for Michael Ward, the expedition doctor. He later climbed Everest twice, once with Lou's twin brother, Jim, the first American to climb the mountain, in 1963 and again with the third Indian expedition in 1965. Rotund and jovial, he made no secret that he did not plan to do it all again. We grew to like and respect the American team and our fears for their inexperience were groundless, for they stayed as a cohesive unit to the end, pushing high up on to the North Face, though they failed to climb to the summit.

The yaks were due on 29th March. In the intervening days we needed to reconnoitre the route to Advance Base and to become more acclimatised. We left on the 25th as Peter recorded:

Thursday, 25th March, 1982: Base Camp to Camp 1½
We're not ones to rush off in the mornings, despite a faintly big plan. Charlie kindly has sorted out the food. Choosing tent partners – a vegetarian, a snorer or someone who won't make breakfast? Eventually chose Joe – Dick and Chris need to get to know each other. Mr Chen, our LO, goes down to Xegur this morning with the jeep – he's not been feeling too good for a number of days – stomach upset. The weather's rather poor today which puts us all off hurrying anyway. Fully

*clad in one-piece Biffo suit plus Gore-tex/Thinsulate salopettes and jacket. I
suppose it's easier to walk when it's cool. The trekking team left the tents and
some gear up there – Chris and Dick don't even have to carry pits, because
they're up there. We become fairly widely spread out. Turn left, see walls of the
prewar Camp 1. I'm carrying Koflachs, wearing KSB 3s. 32lbs. What's that
about a pound of weight on your feet? Starts to snow. After a few hours, find
Dick where the trekking team left their tents. 'Camp 1½.' Dick has a brew
ready, Joe misses the way, then Charlie. Chris goes back to help Adrian.
Eventually all ensconced. The altitude gets me, I can't remember much 'at
height', anyway my writing's wobbly. I'm sharing with Joe – it seems better to
read* Manchu. *Dick and Chris eating gluey tsampa.*

Friday, 26th March: to prewar Camp 2, 6000 metres

*This is only our fourth or fifth day's exercise and here we are carrying over
forty-pound loads from between 5500 and 6000 metres. This morning's weather
still snow. These nights are long, sound sleep for a while then fitful with long
periods of wakefulness – just roll over and try lying the other way. So we
appreciate the lie-in and I read more* Manchu. *Eventually we do pack up and
leave, early afternoon. With Charlie and Adrian out for the walk (they both turn
back fairly soon). Our camp is the other side of the Changtse Glacier, wherever
that is. Guess how we're finding the way up here? We're following telephone
lines! – Chinese, perhaps French, perhaps Japanese, lying on the ground,
occasionally twisted by the wind around ice cliffs and moraines. When Dick took
his trekking group through this way they made a mistake which we don't have to
make again – and they wasted four hours. But they saw Big E – no chance of that
this time. Like yesterday, a few worrying spots for yaks with loose stones on top of
ice. Now we follow those amazing giant blue-green fins of ice in the glacier
(differential melting, of course). This moraine now a broad highway. Find a lot
of stuff – the French must have stopped here and we want to also, since we are
tired. Still snowing lightly. Camp beside a tower of ice like Froggatt Pinnacle –
but at least ice is easier to melt than snow – but everything has a bit of grit in it
because of the winds up here . . . and in the evening the weather clears. Feeling
the altitude and not feeling very hungry and tonight it's intensely cold despite
wearing all my clothes. Cold, starry and still.*

Saturday, 27th March:
prewar Camp 2 to prewar Camp 3 (our Advance Base) and back

*Whilst we're walking up have to remind ourselves how high up we are, higher
than Kohi Mundi*[1] *. . . the sun comes up earlier here than at Base – nine fifteen –
and it is a perfect day. The Yanks seem impressed that we set off in that bad
weather to come up here the other day but – 'do the unexpected' and now we're
vindicated. We shall walk up unladen today – a clear way but high up. Chat.
Chris has very good feelings about this trip, as good as he's ever had about the
team. I say, 'And we all know what we're taking on.' It's been funny listening to*

[1] A 6248-metre peak in Afghanistan Peter climbed in 1972.

them next door. Chris talking a lot but Dick holding his own with his usual devastating one-liners . . . The mountain and glacier are swept clear and hard by winter winds – the glacier is glassy, translucent, hard. We stop often and look up as the Ridge appears in pieces before us (through cloud and gaps in the ice pinnacles). Oh, yes, I managed to finish Manchu *before we left this morning. Looks a very long way – and still winter so clear of snow. Find a good spot from where we can contour to the Raphu La. Here we hope will be our Advance Base. It seems at the moment the highest, bleakest, most windswept place on earth. At first through the Raphu La we can see Pethangtse and then from higher up, Chomo Lonzo with its unclimbed North West Summit that looks like the Dru . . . I don't think this is going to be the most comfortable Advance Base but at least it's high up. We'll have to wear crampons just to walk across to the Raphu La, the ground's so icy! A few prewar tins here (the French camped higher up). But the Ridge continues to make a great line . . . Decided not to have a brew up here – we scuttle off back down to Camp 2, it only takes one and a half hours. Chris has his little tape recorder for the BBC programme and asks for a few comments! He lingers behind to record his own thoughts in whispered ecclesiastical tones. Back at the camp ahead of Chris we chat briefly. 'There's no-one else like him,' says Dick, 'he's unique – always doing something even if it's projecting plans on the route or writing his diary.' Chris has named one nasty-looking tooth on the Ridge 'the Fang' – still a question if we'll find a straightforward way round it. But we'll certainly get some good photos, it being a ridge . . . Difficult to eat properly up here with the unappetising food and altitude – and the time to melt ice also. We'll have to get organised for our Advance Base. Perhaps it'll just have to be a hunter's return at Base. Tonight I start and finish the thriller,* Gorky Park *– it grips me so much I read until half past midnight. I sleep well.*

Sunday, 28th March: prewar Camp 2 to Base Camp

A month today I left Leysin – looking forward to the post but I can wait. I suppose time away depends upon how long you expect to be away and, expecting this to be a long campaign, this last month has gone very quickly – and the next month should see us working our way up the route – and, hopefully, poised . . . It's another lovely still morning, prelude to a windy afternoon blowing up the valley . . . We leave everything except that which we walk about in at camp and set off down. 'The Fang' appears again. It's important to give things names . . . Rapid progress downhill, about four hours, 11.30 to 15.30 with rests and looks. High mountain, looks low here and dry . . . At the East Rongbuk junction we meet two Yanks, the camera man and Mr Warner Bros., they give us a cool sip. Carrying enormous loads. Thank goodness we don't have to do that or prove that. The authors discuss – only Dick not publishing a book this year! Hope they're not reviewed together. Ask Dick if he's thought about Alpine guiding; he thinks he might not be immediately sociable enough . . . Back at Base – the flocks of Alpine Choughs which now live here race off. Some yaks and yak men – the Yanks are shifting their stuff now. Watch for wandering Tibetans; they'll pick up anything you leave around. Tang orange juice (so much better than Rise 'n Shine) – three loaves of Charlie's bread and his cheesecake. A lovely afternoon – I have my first proper wash (except hair) since Xegur. Charlie flies his kite from the frozen lake; from my tent door it looks higher than Everest! Eat a lot.

Monday, 29th March
1900 hours. A pleasant day. Handwriting improving as I acclimatise. Dick spends his hours carving a swan from a block of mahogany and sketching. I write up my diary, wash pants and socks, do a cross section of Big E on the graph using Schneider's map and compose a little poem about Everest's Flag Clouds. Now the sun comes up on the tent at 9.58! After supper the Americans come around and I shall give them this to post . . . a great evening, successful entertainment. Had a long, far ranging chat with Jim Wickwire for about two hours. About K2, Peter Goodwin, Dalai Lama, Charlie Houston, Jim Morrisey's expedition to the East Face of Everest last year which made such a profit, K2 summit view, Namche Barwa and so on. He has a library of 3000 climbing books . . . It was great to talk to someone so interested in the same things – though he is rather intense. They liked the 'I'm a wanker' song. We're a very happy expedition and they absorbed that from us I think. An hilarious time but too stimulating and not a good night's sleep.

The yaks had not yet arrived: it was nobody's fault for things move slowly in Tibet. Our jeep was away in Xegur so we waited, reading and resting. The weather at Base Camp was mixed, usually fine and blustery but very cold. I recorded the temperatures carefully, always having omitted to do so regularly before. Before the sun hit us at about nine forty-five a.m. at Base it was – 12°C both within my tent and in the shade outside. An hour later, within, it would rise to 20°C, although in shade outside it would be only 2°C. Sunset beyond the hills west of Rongbuk was shortly before seven p.m.

On 31st March I strolled down the valley with Chris for half an hour to the first evidence of the highest previous inhabitants, the Rongbuk Nunnery. Perched on the tongue of a huge landslide, its fifty or so dwellings were in ruins, destroyed by man, not rockfalls. A few walls remained with flecks of fresco but hidden away there was a tiny shrine.

A wooden trap in a sandy floor led in the darkness down a flimsy ladder. With a headlamp a simple clay Buddha peered at us through the gloom. Around were some cast figures, old prayer flags, coins and carved slates. A butter lamp was still warm, the low vault smokey. This shrine, easily concealed in a cellar, had escaped destruction and was still in use. Chris and I looked down towards the Rongbuk Monastery a mile or so away and decided to go a little further. Within a few minutes we met thirteen yaks and five yak herders camped by the stream. They greeted us with smiles, some with the old Tibetan custom of pushing forward their tongues, gently, through an open mouth rather than sticking them out like rude children. These were our men and they would meet us next day at Base.

Dusk was approaching so we turned and walked home, more tired than we expected. Chris was relaxed, happy with the team but keen to get moving. We both felt that this expedition, although it might have hidden dangers, contained no personalities in which there lay the seeds of discontent. We knew each other well, knew of our weaknesses, could sniff the signs of irritation or the wish to be alone. There was a fraternal atmosphere, by no means always one of agreement, but one of intuitive understanding. There was much laughter too.

We left in the early afternoon of 2nd April for the prewar Camp 1, tucked round the corner at the end of the East Rongbuk Valley. Travelling together seemed a new experience. Joe filmed the yaks on a steep corner which turns into the East Rongbuk, causing a minor stampede. Peter carried the huge cine tripod and Chris helped with a load of films. An easy walk to the mess of the old French camp site. Peter sat in silent fury with an ice hammer flattening over two hundred empty Camping Gaz canisters, the manufacturer's label advertising in vain 'Leave No Litter' in three languages. We sat, cooked and read a while in the heavy military mess tent that was to be home at Advance Base. We were impressed by our yak herders, a gentle lot who looked after their animals well. They had already shown us a new route to the camp, crossing the ice lake of the glacial stream instead of fighting up the moraines along its left bank.

The next day saw us to the old Camp 2 along the screes of the left bank with a rough track marked with red paint splashes on the rocks by the Japanese. This was a hillside on the move with many red boulders swept away below the route. It looked safe enough, though, until a steep scree slope to a shelf. Here the path had been lost and needed rebuilding for the yaks who, though agile, cut their feet on sharp stones. The Tibetans leapt into action hurling boulders from the slope and creating in minutes a zig-zag path for forty-five metres. Joe and Peter filmed while Adrian and I pushed on.

We would have done better to have waited, for a rattle from above warned of a stonefall. We ran for cover and the air was filled with rocks, several scoring direct hits on my personal bodyguard, a large though unstable boulder. 'They're not aiming at us anyway,' I thought. We hurried along the remaining section, pausing to avoid further stonefalls and arrived in a rather breathless, shaky sweat on a moraine above the previous Camp 1½, mid-way between the prewar Camps 1 and 2. The others came through with no problems but I avoided this section in future by a safe but exhausting scramble in the ice and boulders of the glacial stream.

'Quite acceptable Alpine risks', was the consensus of opinion and I felt a bit wet. It is so often, I thought, on easy ground that accidents happen, on paths, on easy abseils and apparently straightforward glaciers – and I seem to have been involved in more than my fair share, explaining, perhaps, my lack of progress as a hard climber.

This was my first journey along the Rongbuk moraines to Advance Base at 6400 metres. There can be no easier route to this altitude on a great mountain, a gentle walk along moraine, rather monotonous and, apart from the short Rockfall Alley, entirely safe. Above, to the right, towers the wall of Changtse, 7553 metres, a peak opposite the North Face of Everest, rising from the North Col. The northern skyline is of lower peaks, many of them easy and climbed on prewar trips – Kellas's Peak (Ri-ring), Kartaphu and several unnamed 7000-metre peaks. The moraine route winds first between the East Rongbuk and Changtse Glaciers and then, finding the left bank of the East Rongbuk, runs between sérac walls, the edges of two dry glaciers, before turning south and up to Advance Base to look out over the vast expanse of ice which forms the head of the East Rongbuk Glacier, draining the slopes of the Lhakpa La, several smaller northern glaciers, the Raphu La and the séracs of the North Col. Smooth in places, almost like polished glass, there was a fine dust of spindrift blowing across it. In sunlight and calm, a friendly place but in cloud and blizzards, fierce, hostile and forbidding. 'The highest golf course in the world,' Dick said later, when the route was picked out by marker flags across to the Raphu La.

Above, the North East Face of Everest with its crest, the Ridge, towered like a huge sail, furrowed by couloirs of green ice. The scale had been hard to comprehend from photographs for this was a country of giant features with ourselves like Lilliputians beneath it. It was two miles from the Raphu La to the North East Shoulder (8393 metres) and just under a mile further to the summit – great distances at these extreme altitudes. We could see the crest almost in its entirety, beginning as snow and looking easy to 7300 metres. There were then two steep sections, rock buttresses which looked harder – we thought the Chinese had stopped at the first of these in 1964. Thereafter, 2000 metres above us was a series of jagged pinnacles, rock on the north eastern side capped by a crest of snow, the corniced head wall of the Kangshung Face of the eastern side of Everest. The Pinnacles looked hard and dangerous.

Adrian and I helped unload the yaks and left for Base Camp. The work had now begun. It was 4th April.

5: First steps

5th–14th April/Chris Bonington

The site of Advance Base was indeed a bleak spot, a tumbled stony moraine at the edge of the glacier. On one side were crumbling cliffs that guarded the lower slopes of Changtse and on the other our immediate view was barred by a swell of ice. Below, the rocky tongue of the moraine that had provided our highway curled round the corner, leading the eye down the wide open sweep of the glacier. It wasn't a dramatic view. Everest, foreshortened as it was, seemed shapeless and sprawling, hardly the highest mountain in the world, while the peaks on the other side of the glacier, most of them over 7000 metres, were more like snow-clad hills. It had a polar feel to it and reminded me of pictures I have seen of Antarctic ranges. The weather certainly felt Arctic. There was a bitter wind tearing down the glacier and although it was a bright, sunny day, there was no warmth in the sunlight.

Our pile of boxes and kit bags and, for that matter our numbers, seemed puny compared to the vast scale of what was before us. We were already at 6400 metres, yet it did not feel particularly high, perhaps because we were still in the bed of the valley and there was so little snow around us due to the low precipitation on the north side of Everest. As a result we had the luxury of a camp on bare rocks. But once we started shifting rocks for a tent site we were quickly reminded of the altitude, for any sudden exertion caused immediate breathlessness.

Adrian Gordon had borrowed our mess tent from the army in Hong Kong. It was made from heavy canvas and was intended to fit on to the back of a Land-Rover but it was ideal for our purposes, being extremely strong and roomy. Pete dubbed it 'the big Greenie'. It took us most of the afternoon to erect the tent, mooring it to the ground with climbing ropes criss-crossed over the canvas and tied to large rocks. We also built a windbreak in an ineffective effort to shelter the entrance. Inside it was dark and gloomy, with draughts seeking out every chink, but at least it gave us some protection from the elements.

That night there were just three of us at Advance Base, for Joe had returned to our previous camp with Charlie and Adrian to annotate and pack the film he was sending back to Independent Television News in London. We did not bother to put up any other tents but slept in the base tent amongst a mess of food packages, dirty pans and cookers. Dick had walked that day all the way from Base Camp, the ten and a half miles and 1200 metres in height gain, to catch us up. He had stayed behind hoping that our mail would arrive with our jeep but two days had elapsed with no sign of it and he had been forced to walk up empty handed. Even so we were very impressed by the speed of his journey which he had completed in under six hours.

He did not even appear tired, doing as much as any of us to erect the base tent and, that evening, cooking supper. This was all the more commendable since Dick is a vegetarian and he plopped some foil-wrapped meat dishes into the water he was using to cook lentils for himself.

Next morning Pete was feeling ill and unable to eat anything. He complained of pains in his chest and nausea; whether it was altitude or some bug we could not tell, but he managed lethargically to clear a site for his own personal tent, pitch it and then crawled into it to sleep out his malaise.

Dick and I were keen to reach the Raphu La and investigate the approaches to the North East Ridge. We set out just after mid-day, roping up and putting on crampons for the first time on the expedition. I had a feeling of fresh excitement that submerged all the doubts I had held both in the preparatory period and during the approach. At forty-seven, was I too old for this? Could I keep up with the other three? Could I reach the summit without using oxygen? But all this rolled away in anticipation of actually setting foot on the North East Ridge. We took with us a few alloy wands to mark the route and started out. The snow was hard and crisp underfoot, compressed and beaten by the wind. The Raphu La, 6510 metres, seemed little higher than our own Advance Base but first we had to lose height crossing a gentle depression in the glacier. It was a great open sweep of white, unsullied by open crevasses, though the occasional crack in the snow showed that there might be some hidden chasms lurking.

We strode across steadily. I was delighted that I seemed to be fully acclimatised and that I did not need to pause for rests, though we stopped frequently to gaze up at the Ridge to pick out the best route on to it. There was a subsidiary buttress stretching up to a shoulder which was marked on the map as 7090 metres. Pete had suggested that this might be an ideal route, by-passing the lower part of the Ridge and taking us straight up to our first camp on the crest. I had my doubts. It now seemed a long way and, looking at it from close by, we could see dirty streaks of black ice and broken rocky steps barring the way. It did not look easy.

We plodded on, breasting a gentle slope that led towards the col. The rocky head of Chomo Lonzo peered over the crest and then, as we reached the col, everything opened out. The slope before us dropped dizzily out of sight. This was no mountain pass and it was hardly surprising that it had never been crossed for the Kangshung side was steeply glaciated in a series of sérac walls. The Kangshung Glacier itself, 1200 metres below, was dirty rubble-covered ice seamed with open crevasses. Looking down the glacier an array of peaks, most of them unclimbed, even unnamed, stretched into the distance but on the far horizon, some eighty miles away, squatted the great bulk of Kangchenjunga, 8598 metres, third highest mountain of the world. The fact that Pete and Joe had climbed it with Doug Scott in 1979 gave us a point of reference. To its right, dwarfed but nonetheless shapely and steep, was Jannu, 7710 metres, also climbed by friends, Roger Baxter-Jones, Rab Carrington, Brian Hall and Al Rouse, in the autumn of 1978.

The peaks on the southern side of the Kangshung Glacier were fiercely dramatic. Chomo Lonzo, 7790 metres, dominated the horizon for it was closer and more rugged than Makalu, 8475 metres, its taller neighbour. Even closer was the shapely summit of Pethangtse, 6710 metres, which led the eye along and up the great eastern ridge of Lhotse, 8501 metres, whose huge and threatening South East Face jutted into wind-driven clouds. But most impressive of all was the back, or south eastern aspect, of our Ridge which we could just see from the col. The Kangshung Face thrust its way into the cloud base some 1500 metres above us, in a slope that was crazed with erratic fluting and runnels, sérac walls and naked black rock.

The sight was both daunting and immensely exciting. It showed just how serious the North East Ridge was to be, but we hoped to avoid the south eastern side and follow easier slopes on the north west.

We set foot for the first time on the North East Ridge that afternoon. From the Raphu La the slope swelled up like the face of a gigantic wave with the occasional cornice breaking at its crest. At first the angle was easy, around thirty-five degrees, and the snow crisp and hard, giving us a feeling of security as we zig-zagged our way across it. I quickly forgot the intimidating aspect of the other side of the Ridge in the joy of movement, in such superb surroundings. That afternoon we climbed about 200 metres, traversing well below the crest to find a spot where we could gain safe access to the slopes leading to it and thus find a short cut to the Ridge, avoiding the Raphu La.

We did not go far that day; just enough to reassure ourselves of the quality of the snow and the line of the route before dropping down the slope to a point where we could safely cross the bergschrund at its foot. At the bottom we found a good viewpoint from which to pick out the best route to the crest. We favoured a compromise between the subsidiary arête that had attracted Pete and the crest of the Ridge from the Raphu La. Inevitably we worried about the cornices but finally resolved that they were reasonably safe.

Dick and I returned well satisfied with what we had done and seen, though on the way back we discovered that the glacier was not as innocent as it had seemed. What appeared on the surface as little more than a crack opened out into a vast, bell-shaped crevasse whose depth and sides were lost in a black void. We traced our journey back in a wide arc to avoid any risk of avalanche from the flanks of the North East Ridge. This detour had a sting in the tail, however, for there was a gentle though exhausting climb near the end, followed by a long plod to the very edge of the glacier before suddenly our Advance Camp came into sight, tucked away in a hollow of the moraine. Pete and Joe had used the day to erect tents for all of us so that the base tent could be used for living and cooking together.

Next morning the wind howled down the valley ceaselessly so we used it as an excuse to spend the day making our camp slightly more comfortable, draping a tarpaulin over the base tent, making a table of stones inside it for cooking and eating and building windbreaks in front of our personal tents. By evening the camp had at last begun to feel habitable though it was still desperately cold and we never took off our down suits. Feet were chilled and frozen even inside our sheepskin camp boots. We felt very much alone.

We had spent a lot of time both back in England and in the early stages of the expedition poring over photographs, discussing strategy and tactics. Being a team of four ruled out the use of oxygen as a major part of the plan, for we could never have carried the cylinders, each weighing about seven kilos, up to 7900 metres or so. Pete, Joe and Dick wanted to climb the mountain without oxygen, though my own attitude was more ambivalent. I wanted to get to the top of Everest and had fairly serious doubts about my ability to do it without the help of oxygen, which was why I had insisted on bringing a stock of cylinders and masks as far as Advance Base. There was the chance of changing our policy if circumstances suggested it later.

There were two ways we could have tackled the Ridge. One was by conventional siege methods with a series of camps linked by fixed ropes until we had a camp close enough to the summit for one or two to make a summit bid. The other way was to climb the mountain Alpine-style which meant packing our rucksacks at the foot of the mountain with about ten days' food, a tent and all the climbing gear and keeping going, camping and bivouacking on the way. On Everest, Reinhold Messner had used Alpine-style tactics in his incredible solo ascent from Tibet in 1980. He had made a reconnaissance to the North Col but then climbed the mountain in a single push, camping twice on the way up, reaching the summit, getting back to his top camp on the third day and returning to Advance Base on the fourth. Messner was climbing a known route that was comparatively straight-forward. We, however, would be on new ground with the additional problem which we knew from photographs that the principal difficulties started at around 7900 metres and went on up to 8380 metres, over a series of pinnacles that barred the way to the upper part of the Ridge.

It seemed to make sense, therefore, to adopt a compromise between the two approaches, establishing a series of camps – we hoped just two – to the foot of the Pinnacles and then to make an Alpine-style push from this high base with one or more bivouacs up to the summit. We hoped this would enable us to acclimatise on the route itself, coming down for rests at Base or Advance Base, until we were ready to make that summit push. We would only be able to use a little fixed rope because of the problems of carrying it but we were hoping that the lower part of the Ridge would be sufficiently straightforward for us to do without this safeguard. In view of the high winds we had already experienced we were hoping to dig snow caves, certainly as far as the Pinnacles, since they would be more stable, less noisy and certainly very much more restful than tents.

The dawn was clear on 7th April and even the wind had dropped a little. Loading ourselves with a few ropes, deadmen snow anchors and pitons, we set out over the glacier following the line of marker flags that Dick and I had left on our reconnaissance. We kept up a good steady pace, plodding over the ice without a rest until we were just short of the Ridge. I could not help being relieved that Pete and Joe agreed with our assessment of the best route onto the Ridge. We each dumped one of our ski sticks at the foot but carried the second to use in one hand, an ice axe in the other. On this occasion we remained roped, Dick and I on one rope, Pete and Joe on the other.

This, our first sortie, took place three weeks after reaching Base Camp. We were fresh, rested and acclimatised and plodded steadily, moving together in a series of zig-zags up the crisp snow towards the crest of the Ridge. The snow was so crisp and firm it felt very secure as we followed it up to the spine of a subsidiary spur which gave way to broken rock on the other side. A basin of steep snow below the crest of the corniced Ridge led to another spur. It was steep enough to justify moving one at a time and Dick set out to lead the first pitch, taking a line about thirty metres below the crest, where the angle was easiest.

Pete and Joe watched but Pete was unhappy about the line, pointing out that if there was a heavy snowfall the weight of an avalanche could be considerable. Pete favoured a higher line, just below the cornices, and set out to prove his point. He climbed steeply to a small notch in the Ridge. Peering over the brink on the other side he was confronted by a terrifying drop. Sheer flutings of rotten snow clung to steep black rock, dropping away for over 1000 metres into the heavily crevassed and dirty snows of the Kangshung Glacier. It was four rope lengths to the top of the next spur – another rocky spine projecting out of the snow. The next basin looked even steeper than the one we had just climbed, and beyond it was yet another, to bar our way before we reached the top of the shoulder on which we had hoped to set our first camp. I was beginning to tire and announced, 'I don't know what you lot think but I've gone far enough for one day. This is a good spot for a snow cave and I think we should stop here.'

Even as I said it I realised that I was being defensive about my own fatigue, anticipating Pete's drive to achieve planned objectives, particularly when they were well within his own reach. On this occasion, however, I think I was being unnecessarily sensitive for the others readily agreed with me and I suspect that everyone had had enough for that day. I dug into the snow and though it was very compact, it did not seem excessively icy; more important, it seemed deep enough for us to be able to dig out a snow cave. We draped our load of ropes around a rock and started back down, climbing unroped now that we knew the route.

We took one rope down with us and all four of us roped up on the glacier in case there were any hidden crevasses. That evening, still quite fresh, we strode back to Advance Base in just over half an hour. The camp itself was still exceedingly uncomfortable with the gear and food once again a chaotic shambles. The following day dawned blustery and grey so we had another session of clearing up the camp site and preparing climbing equipment, food and cooking gear that we were going to need for our first serious sortie. Once assembled, we assessed it would come to about ten loads, for we now had to start ferrying the rope we would probably need higher up the mountain.

On 9th April, therefore, we set off with our first carry and started to dig out the snow cave. Although I had estimated that this would be straight-forward, it proved much harder than we had anticipated since almost immediately we hit ice. Chipping it away was a long laborious process. Only one person at a time could get into the hole we had dug. He worked flat out for about five minutes and then crawled out to allow the next one in line a turn; and it went on throughout the day.

By late afternoon the cave was barely large enough for two people to squeeze inside. Joe was determined to get everything on film, both inside and out. He crouched down outside the hole, asking Pete to shovel the snow straight at him to get a dramatic effect. Pete did so with such energy that the blade of the shovel shot off the end of the handle, hit Joe in the face, nearly knocking him off his precarious footholds and then bounced down the steep slope, coming to rest about one hundred metres below. It was characteristic of Pete that with simply a mutter of apology to Joe for nearly decapitating him, he immediately set off to retrieve the shovel, cramponing down steep snow, teetering across some exposed rock and then climbing back up without even pausing to rest. We continued digging for an hour or so before descending to Advance Base. We returned the following day with the plan that Joe and Dick, who had drawn the short straws, should stay at our First Snow Cave while Pete and I would carry up loads of food and climbing gear, then return to Advance Base to move up with our personal gear the following day.

On the way back down on 10th April, Pete and I paused on top of the slight spur where we left the single ski stick we used on the lower slopes. It was a magnificent late afternoon with the cloud building up in a huge wall behind us, somehow contained by the barrier of the North East Ridge. The sky to the north was clear, a cold pale blue over the russet folds of the Tibetan plateau.

'You know,' Pete said, 'I really enjoy this business of going up and down the route, slowly getting to know it better. It was like that on Kangch, where we ended up doing the same thing. I find I don't get bored with it. It's getting to know the mountain itself better and better.' I shared his feelings.

The following day, while Pete and I plodded for the third time up to the snow cave, Dick and Joe set off on the next section of the Ridge. There was a fierce wind with the cloud closing in at an early stage. The incline was now steeper, dropping dizzily for 700 metres to the glacier below. Being on new ground they climbed roped, moving one at a time, front-pointing, with ice axe and hammer in either hand. It was a slow, cautious process, and it took them some hours to cross to the security of the broken rocky spur that dropped down to the glacier from the shoulder. They were then able to move together, scrambling over broken rocks, picking their way from one strip of hard snow to the next, to the crest of the Ridge. Visibility was down to a few metres. It was a strange, frightening world of screaming wind and scudding snow, of a slope that dropped precipitously into a boiling cauldron of cloud. And then they reached a point where the snow had peeled away from the rocky Ridge, forming a series of crevassed holes. Joe wondered whether this could be made into the site of a camp but quickly dismissed the idea, for it all seemed too precarious. It was too close, anyway, to our First Snow Cave. Giving the holes a wide berth they picked their way up the Ridge. This now broadened into a whaleback which, but for the thinness of the air and the bitter cold, could have been somewhere in the Cairngorms, contained as they were in the blanketing cloud. They followed the Ridge for nearly a quarter of a mile until, unsure of where they were, they returned.

Pete and I had waited at Advance Base for as long as possible, hoping vainly that Charlie and Adrian would arrive with the yaks and, most important of all, with some mail, for we had now been away from home for over a month without any letters. In Pete's words: 'Our heads turn constantly down the valley, looking for the signs of a few yaks, a few welcome black heads with wide spaced eyes that glow from a great distance in the torch light. So we dawdle and reluctantly pack up and leave at three p.m. after watching the lads on the Ridge; wondering if they're doing the right thing – usually it's best to go as near the crest as possible.'

But there was no sign of the yaks, so we set off back up to join the others. When our small cave was filled with bodies there hardly seemed room for four. I crawled in last and settled into the routine of snow cave living, unrolling my foam sleeping mat, taking off my overboots and boots, brushing each free of loose snow, then crawling into the welcoming sleeping bag to start cooking. One of the advantages of a snow hole is that there is always plenty of snow available in the walls to melt for drinks, though here it was so hard that we needed the ice axe to chip it away.

We had only been separated for a day and yet it was good to be a foursome again, immensely exciting to hear what Dick and Joe had seen and what they thought of our prospects. One of the great advantages of digging snow holes rather than pitching tents, quite apart from the great security and comfort, was that we were always together and could therefore discuss everything. It meant that there was little danger of any kind of schism within the team and that the pairing always remained flexible. We could thoroughly talk over our plans for the climb. It was important that we all agreed to the general principles of our approach. Inevitably there were frequent differences about immediate tactics but these we were able to mull over until we came to a conclusion with which we could all agree.

There was also an affectionate badinage that helped hold us together and defused any tension or argument. It was born from previous trips and a mutual liking and respect for one another. I had known Pete since our expedition to the South West Face of Everest in 1975 but it was on Kongur the previous year that we had come to know each other really well. This was even more the case with Joe for I had shared a tent and climbed with him throughout that expedition. I had first been on an expedition with Joe to K2 in 1978 but the expedition had ended so prematurely when Nick Estcourt had been killed in an avalanche that I had hardly got to know him, and had even disliked him for his constant questioning of every decision. It was a mistrust that was probably mutual, but on Kongur we came to know and like each other, establishing a steady, easy relationship. Although Dick was a friend of Joe and Pete, I had not met him before this expedition. But I got on so well with Pete and Joe I felt I could trust their judgement. With Dick this certainly proved the case. Quiet and thoughtful, and lacking worldly ambition, he unobtrusively got on with any work that needed doing. All too often it was he who cooked the evening meal, went out to get ice to melt for water or did the washing up. Pete commented in his diary: 'Chris thinks Dick is saint-like – makes him feel quite humble.'

By the time all four of us were in our sleeping bags it was a tight squeeze inside the cave. The entrance was blocked by rucksacks but even so the insidious spindrift found its way in. With both stoves going and the entrance blocked, the temperature quickly rose above freezing and, as a result, a steady trickle came down from the roof. Even so it was much more comfortable than a tent. Although the wind was raging outside it was silent within. There was a feeling of cocoon-like security in this tight little cave.

Next morning we were slow in getting ready for the day. There was an element of Lifemanship in trying to avoid being the first pair out of the cave. Pete commented:

Had hoped they'd show the 'newcomers' the way but they don't seem too keen, so I lead off and belay on an ice axe. Chris follows very slowly and so I offer to do the leading so that he can recover in between rope lengths. Eventually we reach the little rocky ridge running up to Point 7090 metres but Chris is depressed at how slow he is going. 'I'll do all I can to support you on this climb but . . .' and I tell him to shut up – we've a long campaign ahead with plenty of time for all of us to fade and recover. He gets a burst of energy and it is all I can do to keep up with him to Point 7090.

I was able to keep in front, roped up but moving together, once we had reached the crest of the Ridge. It was strange how strength ebbed and flowed. Once on the crest the gaping holes on the south east side of the Ridge no longer seemed so threatening. Nevertheless, none of us fancied the thought of trying to use them for shelter. It was easy walking, crampons crunching into firm snow, but the very ease of it made the altitude all the more noticeable; we were now over 7100 metres. I set myself a steady rhythm of fifty steps and then a rest, found I was able to keep ahead of the others and was childishly pleased about it. I reached Joe and Dick's previous high point where there was a little pile of rope tucked into a hollow in the snow, added some of my load and continued up the slope. By this time the cloud had closed in and the wind was gusting fiercely. Just before setting out that morning Dick, whose eyesight was so much better than any of ours, had picked out the tiny black dots of the yaks arriving at Advance Base. Pete and I had left a note asking Charlie and Adrian to open up the radio as soon as they arrived. While Pete and I were starting the route, Joe was trying to contact them and eventually got through to hear the welcome news that the mail had arrived and that each one of us had several letters.

We were now heading for what looked like the first real difficulties on the climb, a steep step in the Ridge, and we wanted to get our next snow hole as close as possible to it. We also had to find a bank of snow sufficiently deep in which to dig a cave. We found what we hoped would be a suitable spot in a slight dip in the Ridge, dumped the ropes we had carried up and started back down. It had taken us five and a half hours to reach this point. That night I could manage to eat hardly anything. It was Pete's turn to cook and he had made chilli con carne from a freeze-dried packet, spiced up with extra chilli powder and garlic. Normally it was the tastiest of all the freeze-dried food but that night neither of us could force down more than a few mouthfuls. Were we building up a resistance to the uniform bland flavour of freeze-dried food or was it simply the altitude? Whichever it was, we were only absorbing a few hundred calories each day yet were expending several thousand. Fatigue was beginning to set in and it was Joe who suggested that we should carry only light loads up to our high point until we had finished the snow cave.

We had returned unroped the previous day, so now set out independently, each at his own pace, without the worry of delaying one's partner. Dick was away first and I quickly dropped behind, needing many more rests than the previous day, plodding up in misery of effort. Were the others feeling the same strain? Joe had a racking cough and was sometimes coughing up blood. But he also had that hard, self-contained sense of discipline and never complained. Perhaps he was feeling just as bad as I but had a greater tolerance to suffering and pushed himself on where I sank into the snow for a rest. Pete, who appeared to have an inexhaustible strength, plodded up the Ridge with what to me seemed an effortless ease, and yet he also had his doubts:

A dullness seems to come over me at altitude. It is so difficult to think about the past or about any aspects of life – beyond the summit, staying alive, little hypochondrias. I try to remember what it's like to feel normal, to be able to concentrate on words, thoughts and ideas (though conversation is stimulating and wide-ranging on this climb). How long we've been at it already – so long – and so long, so long to go. Do I really enjoy it? However much I look around and try to absorb and wonder, try to keep my eyes open, the thought, 'How much of this climb we have yet to do; will I be able to match up to it?' threatens to overwhelm me all the time.

Pete and Dick arrived first at the site of the Second Snow Cave and probed the hard snow with a ski stick to find a suitable spot. By the time I got there half an hour later there was a hole deep enough to crawl into and a cascade of dirty snow, with lumps of ice and grit, being thrown out between Dick's legs. He was like a terrier down a rabbit hole.

We tunnelled away through the afternoon, each taking turns in the hole. After we had been at it for a couple of hours and had a chamber that was barely large enough for one, we hit a wall of shattered rocks. There were three choices; find another spot and start again, bring up tents and use these or just carry on and mine away the rocks. After some discussion we decided on the latter since there seemed no better site for a cave and we had already committed so much time and effort to this one. By mid-afternoon there was just room for two people to work inside. Fortunately the rock was already shattered by frost and could be prised and levered from a bed of close-packed fragments. Even so there was obviously a lot more work to be done before all four of us could move in.

Pete commented:

It's cold and bleak and windy outside; Dick's first to voice the obvious fact that there's not enough work for four at a time up here. I suggest that Dick and I stay, but Joe says: 'Why you?' Chris sets off down alone; I do a bit of digging but then Joe and Dick say I should follow him – 'You know what his route finding is like.' I did promise Wendy I would look after him, and so I rush off down and catch him up as he's leaving the rock rib below Point 7090 – and take over the track finding in the cloud and fresh snow fall.

Certainly all the alpine guiding I've done has helped me walk on snow, without facing inwards with two ice tools all the time, but familiarity with this ground must not breed over relaxation – it's a long bouncy drop down to the glacier.

That night back in our First Cave, we discussed strategy. I was all for going back down for a rest the next day. The thought of mail from home as much as my growing fatigue was a strong influence. Dick, quietly determined, was adamant that we must finish the cave before going down. It made sense and I resigned myself to another day of effort, though that night I could only force down a few mouthfuls of the vegetarian meal of cheesy mashed potato with sweet corn that Pete had prepared.

At least I was bright in the mornings and uncurled myself at about seven when it was still dark, to turn round to get my head at the same end as the entrance. I pushed Pete's slumbering feet up out of the way and shook the pan and stove free from the chill dusting of spindrift that covered everything at the bottom of the snow hole. A struggle with the lighter and soon the stove was melting the snow for the first brew of the morning. It was a slow, painful sequence. It never took less than three hours to make three brews, to force down some cereal and perhaps some biscuit and cheese, then to crawl out of the warmth of the sleeping bag and grapple with boots and overboots ready for another day's toil.

It was a fine, windless morning, the best so far, and we got going at half past ten, our earliest so far. I was full of good intentions and away first. I cramponed up the snow just beyond the cave but I had no strength in me and had to use every ounce of will power to make each step. It was not so much a case of breathlessness but rather a heavy lethargy that had taken over my limbs. I knew I could not make another journey without having a real rest. So I turned round and dropped back to the cave where Pete was just putting on his crampons. I told him I would have to leave them to it for the day and go down by myself. There seemed no point in waiting for them in the cave and I was prepared to risk crossing the glacier without a rope, as much as anything to get the letter I longed for.

I set off down. It was so easy once I started descending. I could not help feeling guilty. My logic told me that if I was to last the course I would have to nurse myself, yet I hated doing it, hated admitting that I no longer had the stamina the others had.

As I dropped down the other three climbed towards the Second Cave. It had been our plan to return to Advance Base after putting in a day of work. They took only two hours to reach the previous high point and spent the rest of the day mining the rock and snow. Pete commented:

I slowly put on my oversuit and start digging. It's a bit limited because Dick has the only good axe for chopping and the snow and rocks are getting a bit hard for the shovel . . . We had a full afternoon's work at nearly 7300 metres, with those familiar little hallucinations as we chop. Nicer to be working inside than emptying the long approach trough because of the afternoon wind. We're all feeling the strain now of many days on the trot of hard work without much food . . . and, most worrying, we've all got cold feet.

Around five p.m. we come to a stop – had enough digging really for today; there is still quite a bit of work to do but that can wait till next time. Once more snow has fallen; what tracks are visible are tricky to follow – place axe at every step.

We pile into the snow cave and leave most of the gear, including down suits, here. Dick, last to arrive, smells as much as I do in the enclosed space as he changes. Joe sets off down first. I wait for Dick and follow him along the 'Ramp' cornice.

Meanwhile I had reached Advance Base. It was a delight seeing Adrian and Charlie, to be pampered and spoilt with a soup made from fresh vegetables and bread cooked that day in a make-shift oven, but most exciting of all was the prospect of letters from home. Charlie handed over a little pile to me. There was one I wanted and needed above all, the one from Wendy. At a glance at the envelopes no sign of her handwriting but maybe it was in the typewritten one. I tore them open, a sense of growing desolation overwhelming me. There were letters from my secretary, from friends at home but there wasn't one from Wendy. I had noticed the effects on others when they failed to get letters from home. I was now experiencing it at first hand. It was particularly hard that evening when the others, desperately tired but fulfilled and satisfied with what had been a long weary day, opened their letters and exchanged news from home. Pete noticed: 'Chris has no letter from Wendy. He's quiet all evening and reads while we chat.'

I went to bed early, to my cold little tent and although I tried to rationalise that a letter could have been delayed or could have just missed this post, although I was secure in Wendy's love, I nonetheless wrote a bitter, hurtful torrent of words that, of course, would reach home weeks later, out of all sequence with what had happened, and after Wendy had written me several letters whose love and reassurance were to do more than anything else to keep me going.

Next morning the sun warmed the tent and we each lay cocooned in our sleeping bags and thoughts until Charlie and Adrian came round with mugs of steaming tea. It was good to be cosseted, good to be back in the comparative luxury of Advance Base and we had the satisfaction of knowing the Second Snow Cave at 7256 metres was nearly ready for the next foray.

6: The Second Snow Cave

16th–23rd April/Chris Bonington

We were sorry to see Adrian and Charlie leave for Base Camp two days later. It was not just cupboard love. True they looked after us, preparing delicious meals, chiding us for not eating more, collecting ice from the glacier, washing up, but it was their company that was most precious. Charlie, relaxed and amusing, helped us to escape from the tense seriousness of our task, while Adrian, much quieter, lent reassuring support. I could not help thinking of what it must have been like for Pete and Joe on Changabang in 1976, for they had been on their own for three months while climbing its West Wall. There had been no respite from each other's company and the fact that they had come through this had given their relationship a particular strength, though they often bickered at each other like an old married couple. There was a strong element of competition in their relationship, and this was perhaps getting stronger as they expanded their ambitions and talents in writing. Each wanted to write the book describing this expedition. So many mountaineering partnerships and friendships have been destroyed by the pressures of fame and ego, and yet I had a feeling that this particular one had a durability that could withstand these stresses.

Dick's relationship with both Pete and Joe was slightly different. There was no question of competition, for Dick's ambitions seemed entirely within himself, as a test or perhaps a quest to discover what he could achieve for his own fulfilment. He did not, as they did, need to communicate his experience to a wider audience.

The three days went all too quickly. We frequently gazed up at the ramparts of the North East Ridge, focusing on the two buttresses immediately above the Second Snow Cave. These looked as if they would present the first serious difficulties of the climb. Through the telescope we could see what appeared to be a steep snow gully going through the First Buttress, but the Second Buttress seemed to present a rocky barrier stretching across the full extent of the Ridge.

Our last day, 17th April, was spent in sorting out food and climbing gear for our second foray. We hoped not only to climb the two steps but also to establish a third snow cave on the conspicuous shoulder just below the Pinnacles, which we thought would be the crux of the climb. Next day we spent a dilatory morning finishing off our packing, unconsciously delaying the end of our relaxation and the moment of toil.

The wind was as cruel as ever, picking up clouds of fine snow, as we trailed across the glacier. I had taken the precaution of being in front so that

I could set a steady pace. The slopes leading up to the crest of the Ridge, blown clear of snow, were once again firm and secure as we zig-zagged up them, a ski stick in one hand, an ice axe in the other.

We had left a foam mat pinned in place across the entrance of the First Snow Cave, so only a little spindrift had leaked in. We were able to install ourselves quickly and settle back into the routine of high mountain living. There was still a lot of food, fuel and climbing gear to be ferried up to the Second Snow Cave and more work to be done to make it habitable. Pete and I attended to that the next day, descending to our First Cave at night.

Pete describes the evening ritual:

Life inside the cave: Chris and I swop positions and cooking duties. It's warm in here, five degrees above freezing sometimes, with condensation dripping from the ceiling. Warmest between Dick and Chris – Chris has now taken the hints about animal farm noises, and he coughs and clears his nose inside his sleeping bag . . . sleep is getting a bit better (avoiding pills, unlike Chris and Joe) but appetite not much. Funny how an 'us and them' mentality, based on cooking pairs, comes out even when four of us are all crammed together in the cave.

Managing to keep regular (though put it off an hour or so yesterday 'cos of the wind). This entrance is a bit short, so some spindrift problems, but it's a good cave and a haven, though there is not much of a ledge outside. We can only get down bland foods, usually powdered potato and cheese, spiced up with onions, garlic and chilli.

The following morning we loaded up our sacks and set out for the Second Snow Cave. This time we were going to stay. The previous day, I had travelled light, something noticed by the others, which meant that I now had an extra quantity of food as well as my sleeping bag and spare clothes. We all tended to watch each other to ensure that work was fairly divided.

Pete observed:

Chris leaves behind some of his Gaz canisters but is spotted: 'You can't get away with anything on this trip,' he says cheerfully and loads them into his sack. Dick's away first again. He's always willing to have a go first, but looks tense and uncertain and ponderous on steepish ground . . . I usually try thirty paces at a time up here, but it's hard work with a load. Dick reaches the snow cave first and plunges in and starts hacking. He gets crabby around 7300 m sometimes and makes a comment that I should start clearing the debris he's made, but I'm hacking a big platform outside on which to stack the polythene bags of food we carried up yesterday.

Eventually all four of us are hacking and clearing. The slopes and fall line outside are stained with the mud, rock chips and dust from our excavations. We can cut very near the surface because the sugary snow-ice is so hard. Joe is a good shovel hacker . . . one rock is particularly big and stubborn and I declare war on it. Joe eventually shifts it using an ice hammer as a lever. Dick gets stroppy about this misuse of an ice tool until he realises that it is not his own. Joe is really funny on this trip and rarely misses an opportunity to tease.

Joe Tasker

Adrian Gordon

Chris Bonington

Peter Boardman

Dick Renshaw

Charlie Clarke

The Potala was once thought to be the highest building in the world

opposite: Base Camp, with Changtse and Everest in the background

Entrance to the Norbulingka, Summer Palace of the Dalai Lamas

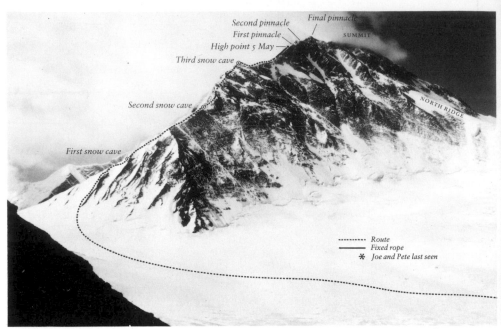

Second pinnacle
First pinnacle
High point 5 May
Third snow cave
Final pinnacle
SUMMIT

Second snow cave

NORTH RIDGE

First snow cave

·········· Route
———— Fixed rope
✳ Joe and Pete last seen

above right: The Kangshung Face from the Raphu La

below right: Pete and Joe below the First Snow Cave, with Chomo Lonzo beyond, the Kangshung Glacier below and Kangchenjunga on the far horizon

below: Charlie at work

At the Second Snow Cave we hit rock

opposite: Chris climbing a steep snow gully on the First Buttress

Our yak herders treated their beasts with enormous care and consideration

One of us had to stay outside in the cold to clear the rubble from the entrance and kick it down the slope. It was Dick's turn when, once again, he picked out the tiny black specks of the yaks returning to Advance Base. Even though Charlie and Adrian were so far away and could not possibly do anything to help us in an emergency it was reassuring to know that they were back. That night they brought us up-to-date on the Falkland Islands crisis and told us the news we were really waiting for, that there was some more mail for all of us.

There is always a tendency to declare a snow cave large enough when it barely is and this occasion was no exception. We were tired and cold and longed to creep into our warm sleeping bags. The prized position in any snow cave is obviously as far as possible from the entrance. Not only is this the warmest spot but it also means that no-one crawls over you. I suggested that we drew lots, but Dick, with typical selflessness, volunteered to take the uncomfortable door position. I'm afraid the rest of us took no persuading. Joe, still cooking with Dick, was next in line, then me, and Pete was on the inside since it was his turn to cook for us.

While Pete and I had a comfortable night, next morning Dick was almost completely covered in snow from spindrift blown in from the partly blocked entrance. He was cold and shivery and just lay still in a stupor. I could not help wondering why Dick had not done more to protect himself from the snow, even if it had meant waking the rest of us. Pete felt the same way: 'To me this is stupid silent suffering, since he had access to two closed-cell foam mats and all those polythene bags full of food with which he could easily have blocked off the entrance and kept warm. There seemed to be a touch of "This high altitude is suffering, therefore I must suffer," about it all. I say this to Chris later, but he is much more tolerant than I am.'

We were all sluggish that morning and talked around the problem. The snow cave was so uncomfortable, that I suggested two should remain behind to do something about it while the others went out and attempted our First Buttress.

'But what are two people going to do all day here?' asked Pete.

'There's a lot of work in just making that ruddy passageway fairly snow proof. And just getting all the food sorted out, and when they've done all that they can have a brew, they can lie down, they can dream,' I replied.

'And read *Daniel Martin*,' said Pete.

'They can read *Daniel Martin* as long as they let me have it back.'

'Well, I don't mind what I do but I do think it is very important that this place is sorted out. It's just ridiculous lying here covered in snow all night,' said Joe.

'I wouldn't know about that,' said Pete from the security of his space at the end of the cave.

'I know. You've got no spindrift on you. This is from the last half hour, not from all night,' said Joe.

'I'm having a marvellous time over here; I've no idea how much you lads are suffering over there,' said Pete.

'I'm glad you appreciate it, I'm glad you are seeing the luxury of your situation,' replied Joe.

'Well,' I suggested, 'I think it just makes life simpler if two people know that their function in life is to get this place sorted out . . .'

'And get smacked on the bottom if it's not done,' riposted Joe.

'By Daddy Boardman,' I said, to keep it light.

'Well,' said Pete, 'I'm going to check what page Bonington's on in *Daniel Martin*.'

'Let's draw straws for who does what,' I suggested. 'I think two people should have the function to make this place liveable in.'

'Do you agree with that, Joe?' asked Pete.

'Yeah, but I'm not sure about drawing straws. I think the people who are better at doing snow caves should do the snow caves.'

'I'm inclined to agree to that,' I interjected.

'I'm not saying this because I think I'm better at snow caves, I'd just as soon go on the hill.'

'I know I'm not very practical,' I observed. 'I'm not very good at that sort of thing. Dick's very good at sorting out snow caves because he's practical. I would say, as a suggestion, Dick and Joe are both rather good at it. Pete's very good at charging over the hills and I'm a kind of a dead weight to hold him back.'

'Don't you agree, Pete?' checked Joe.

'Yes.'

'I mean, would you prefer to stay here or . . .'

'No. I'll go with the flow. I'm just feeling guilty that I had such a comfortable night over here.'

And so it was decided. Pete and I were to push the route out, while Joe and Dick improved the snow cave. This was how most of our decision-making took place and it worked well.

It was exciting to venture on to new ground next morning and I found the fatigue that had almost overwhelmed me the previous day vanish with the prospects of some real climbing. As always the distance to the foot of the First Buttress was much further than we had anticipated. It was up a gentle wave of snow and we did not bother putting on the rope. I was even able to keep ahead of Pete as we plodded over the crisp surface towards a rocky prow that barred our way on the crest of the Ridge. A traverse over easy-angled, slabby rock led towards a snow field which, in turn, led up to the gully which we hoped would take us through the Buttress at about 7300 metres. Looked at head-on it seemed very steep.

We continued to climb solo up increasingly steep snow-ice to a small, rocky island. It was time to rope up but the rock was very compact and there were no cracks for pitons. I ended up putting a dead man snow anchor into the snow just above the island, and Pete started to front point up towards the rocks above. It was a lovely, cold, clear day, and I had time to gaze around me. The North Col was far below, the summit of Changtse seemed almost level with us, and we could see over the peaks guarding Everest to the north and east, to the rolling purple hills of the Tibetan plateau, broken by the occasional white cap of some distant snow peak.

Pete's progress was slow. All movement is at that altitude. On reaching the rocks he probed around trying to find a suitable crack for a piton and eventually found one. He then led on up the side of the rocks until the rope had nearly run out. I followed, using my Petzel ascendeur for security. My turn to lead. Once in it, the gully did not seem quite as steep as it had done from below; the average angle was probably around sixty degrees, but there were bulges that were considerably steeper.

My progress also was slow, but the climbing was enthralling. Fatigue was banished not just by the risk of falling but by the fascination of breaking new ground, of working out a route, of assessing the security of the deep packed snow. It took me over an hour to run out fifty metres of rope. To Pete the time crawled, but for me it raced by. I had nearly reached the end, was half way up the gully and could see a sloping rock ledge to one side of it with some hairline cracks running into it. Just enough for a knife-blade piton. I tapped one in and wondered whether it would hold Pete when he came up. He reached me and led on up the gully. The angle began to relent and he climbed out of sight. Another long pause, a distant hammering and it was my turn to move once more. Pete had gained the top of the First Buttress and had hammered an angle piton as an anchor into a crack beneath a huge boulder just below the crest of the Ridge. We crouched in the shelter of the rock and nibbled some chocolate before pulling out on to the Ridge itself.

'You know,' I said, 'that's the first time we've actually been on the same rope together.'

'Not quite,' Pete replied. 'Don't you remember when I came up to your place before the '75 trip to be vetted. We did a climb then.'

'What was it?' I asked.

'Haste Not, on White Ghyll in Langdale.'

Broken rock and ribbons of snow led across towards the Second Buttress. It would have been good to look over the other side of the ridge to the east, but it was now getting late and we were tired. We cached the remaining rope under a rock and started back down. It had been an immensely satisfying day with some real progress to show for it.

Back at the Second Snow Cave, the other two had also achieved a lot. The entrance was now guarded by blocks cut out of the hard snow, with a door made from a sleeping mat to stop the spindrift blowing in. They had seen us coming down and had a brew ready. That night it was my turn to cook and next morning Pete and I could laze away the early hours, for it was to be Joe and Dick's turn to go out in front to force the Second Buttress. We were to follow carrying more ropes and climbing gear.

It was eleven thirty before Dick and Joe were ready to start. We followed an hour later but caught them up on the first fixed rope. It was a much warmer, hazy morning, with almost no wind. The mist drifted over the Ridge, softening its outline. It was possible to rest without becoming chilled to the bone. Pete even dropped off to sleep at the top of the First Buttress whilst waiting for me. We picked up the gear we had left behind the previous day and added it to the ropes we had carried up from the Second Snow Cave. I seemed to have used up my quota of energy the previous day and dragged behind the others whilst Pete stormed on, quickly catching them up. They were now on the Second Buttress, and had found a gangway that cut through it. It was little more than scrambling over loose rock, but they left a rope in place to ensure a safe descent.

On reaching the top of the Buttress at 7620 metres, they anchored the rope and carried on for a short distance, but soon it began to snow heavily. The top of the shoulder could only be glimpsed through the flurries and it was impossible to pick out the best route to it. As usual it was Pete who was keen to push on even so.

'Come on, lads, where's the determination? Really we are going to have to get a grip of this route soon. D-day's not just a build-up on the South Coast, we've got to go on the offensive.'

'That's all very well,' replied Joe, 'but there's a bloody great smoke screen and we can't see where the hell we're going. There's no point pushing on blind.'

Pete comments in his diary: 'The Falkland Islands crisis and all the war books on this expedition, combined with living at close quarters with ex-Sandhurst Chris and ex-Gurkha Adrian, have given a lot of war and battle discussions to this trip – all, it must be said, part of the wide ranging political conversation.'

But the flurries of snow quickly brought us back to the qualities of the North East Ridge of Everest. As I reached the top of the second fixed rope they were already returning and by the time I had dumped my load they had vanished in the enveloping snow. There were no tracks, just the glimpse of a flag which marked the high point of the previous day. The sensation was strange; I could have been coming down Striding Edge in a Lakeland blizzard. There was no point of reference except my own exhaustion, a leaden lethargy which made each physical effort supremely difficult.

To my surprise, I caught up with the others at the top of the first fixed rope. I came upon them suddenly, as I rounded the huge boulder to which the rope was anchored. There was a sense of alarm amongst them for Pete had just had a very narrow escape. He had arrived first and had clipped a karabiner and piton brake on to the fixed rope. He was about to lean back to start the abseil, and had just grasped the rope, when the piton anchoring it pulled out in his hands. Had this happened when he had his full weight on it he would almost certainly have fallen backwards and off the end of the rope to his death. This time we had been very lucky. By the time I joined the others they had put in two dead men snow anchors and Pete was again ready to descend. At the end of the fixed rope we had to traverse the slabby rocks, now covered in a layer of treacherous snow. Pete, perhaps shaken by his narrow escape, suggested we needed a fixed rope here but there was none available so Joe simply walked across. Pete followed with uncharacteristic caution, slipping and fumbling. He shouted at Joe heatedly and they had a short slanging match which seemed to release some of the tension.

That night in the Second Cave we were all tired and subdued. The following morning we had a discussion of what we should do next which verged on the acrimonious. Even Pete wanted a day off since he and I had now been on the go for five days without a rest.

A morning with some suppressed anger from me. Not much sign of determination or movement from Joe and Dick. Chris finds a diplomatic way of saying these things. Perhaps we are running out of guts and drive and we need to go down for a rest – down to Base Camp this time. Joe sees the strategic sense of this. But we haven't even seen the Pinnacles from close up. The weather's not helping of course, clouding up in the afternoons and obscuring the view.

Dick proposes staying up, which irritates me a bit because I've been rather disappointed with his dwindling dynamism up here . . . I slowly see the sense in Chris's arguments; he comes up with a clever solution to Joe's now out-dated let's-go-light-with-just-a-shovel strategy – to put two people up there with a tent and try to dig the snow cave from that, so alleviating the need to travel backwards and forwards from the Second Cave with all the accompanying waste of energy.

The discussion lasted the better part of the morning. I was very aware that it was I who tended to call a halt first but I suspect that this acted as a useful counterbalance to Pete's forceful drive which was due in part to the fact that he was probably by far the strongest of us. The close nature of Joe and Pete's relationship meant it was also a competitive one in which neither of them admitted weakness to the other. On Kongur the previous year, I had on occasion felt that Joe had welcomed some of the arguments for delay I had put up, even though he would not have been prepared to initiate such an argument himself.

We eventually decided to go down for a good rest at Base Camp and then follow my plan on our return, to carry a tent up to the shoulder at 7850 metres and for two of us to sleep up there and dig the snow cave. It was mid-day before we were ready to move. We had to take stock of our supplies of food, fuel and climbing equipment, barricade the cave so that it would be habitable and mark it so that we could find it on our return.

It started to snow as we set off. At first it was easy enough, just walking down the crest of the Ridge to Point 7090, but below that the angle steepened and the piled fresh snow was close to the critical point of avalanching. Joe and Dick roped together and, climbing one at a time, set out across the slope. Pete and I were still climbing unroped. We had no choice for we had brought only one rope down with us. It was slow, nerve-racking climbing with the constant threat of a slab of snow breaking away around or above us. It took three hours to get back to the First Snow Cave and another two to reverse the steep slopes below, but the angle then eased and we were able to take the rope off and climb independently down the lower slopes. Even here, though, there was a threat of avalanche and there was no real relaxation until we were back on the glacier.

Although there was now little danger, it was snowing hard and we could only just see the ghostly shape of the next marker wand in this featureless, grey-white world. Dick took the lead of our camel train and we plunged through the white, pausing at each marker to search for the next. Once we set out hesitantly from a wand into the void and suddenly realised, from the way the wind had changed, that we had probably gone in a circle. We retraced our steps, found the last wand and tried again, this time glimpsing a flag over the brow of a slight rise. We were back on track. Advanced Base seemed lonely and derelict. We missed Charlie and Adrian's warm greetings, cups of tea and soup and the friendly cosseting we needed after those days on the hill.

They had obviously left for Base Camp in a hurry. But where was the mail? We lit a stove for a brew and started searching. Surely Charlie and Adrian had not taken it back down with them. The thought of setting off tomorrow for Base Camp leaving our precious letters undiscovered up here was almost unbearable. We angrily searched both the communal 'greenie' tent and all our personal tents several times over but there was still no sign of any letters. It was now dark. Dick had quietly got down to organising our meal and, in looking for ingredients, found the precious bag of mail in one of the food boxes outside the tent. There were letters for all of us. I had three, warm fresh loving ones from Wendy, telling of the day-to-day events at home. I felt remorse for my previous angry and reproachful words to her. We spent the evening happily reading our mail, eating and drinking endless cups of tea and coffee. Tomorrow we were going down to Base Camp; it felt as if we were going back to civilisation.

7: Of yaks and men

5th–25th April/Charles Clarke

For nearly two months after establishing Advance Base Adrian and I lived at a pace very different to that of the four climbers. We had, of course, a task to fulfil, to support the team by keeping the stream of supplies moving to Advance Base, by coping with illness and looking after four tired men when they returned. We also had plans of our own which we rarely discussed, lest they appeared to dilute the climb.

Base Camp was a lonely windswept place as we trudged in on 5th April. The Americans had all set out for the North Face, our trekkers had been gone two weeks. The Chinese staff seemed miserable and many hadn't been well. Mr Chen, the liaison officer and the senior Chinese official with us, had already been taken to hospital in Xegur. Our jeep driver, Mr Cheng, was in Lhasa and so was Dawa, the Tibetan truck driver. Mr Wang, the cook, was demoralised. Mr Yu, the interpreter and thus our only linguistic link with anyone, was, however, pleased to see us. There was no outside news of interest (apart from what sounded like a minor problem in the Falkland Islands) and I felt sorry for the Chinese during their lonely vigil at Base Camp. Apart from Mr Chen none had any personal interest in mountaineering and their work, solely at Base Camp, was monotonous. Western travellers such as ourselves have an inquisitive mentality, an interest, however fitful, in anything unusual, so that each day seems to have only half the waking hours we need for fulfilment. Such was my attitude to Tibet and the Everest region but this was not shared by the Chinese. They were far from home in a country they did not find fascinating. They had to endure cold, hardship and boredom. Yet our Chinese staff worked very hard and consistently. If their ambivalence towards Tibet sometimes angered us, their true worth and feelings were exemplified by patience and, when tragedy occurred, both by humanity and enthusiasm to help in any way. I often wondered how I would feel being an English liaison officer on a Chinese expedition to Northern Ireland.

While the yaks rested for three days among the barren moraines around Base Camp, Adrian and I set about exploring our surroundings. With a file of prewar photographs from the Royal Geographical Society and a set of hand-coloured slides lent by Jack Noel of the 1924 Expedition there was a possibility of finding relics from the past. Where was the old British Base Camp? Where was the memorial left to Mallory and Irvine? Where were the former treasures of Rongbuk? Was there any wildlife in these treeless hills?

We first looked for the prewar Base Camp. One moraine mound looked like another but by aligning the photographs with views of Everest and Changtse we found a flattish area tucked away in the rocks with some old tent sites, a few tins and broken wooden poles. This was clearly the old camp site, and a better and more sheltered spot than our own. The account of the 1924 Expedition relates how, following the loss of Mallory and Irvine, Howard Somervell and Bentley Beetham supervised the construction of a memorial cairn, originally over two metres high. This fine monument with the twelve names of those who had lost their lives before the 1924 accident, was badly damaged by the time the British re-visited Everest in 1933. Little at all remained of it by the last expedition in 1938. There seemed almost no chance of finding it. Adrian and I wandered around turning over rocks and then set off for the crest of a prominent moraine. There indeed was a minute shrine, a disused pot of ashes within a tiny cairn. Our initial hopes went unrewarded – there were no slates, no carvings and no names. Perhaps it was the tomb of a hermit who once lived high in the Rongbuk Valley, the ruins of whose house we had seen. Disappointed we sauntered down the moraine. I kicked over a slate fragment and the light fell on it obliquely, throwing a shadow around the numerals '192'. I felt it must refer to a 1920s expedition. Thus encouraged, we turned up further shards. 'MA . . ., SHER . . . EMBA . . .' A few yards away were larger slates, at the side of an old fire and here was a twenty-kilo slab, the broken headstone of the monument which had once read, '. . . IN MEMORY OF THREE EVEREST EXPEDI-TIONS'. We pieced together as much as we could and built a fresh cairn. I wrote rather laconically to David Newbigging that I thought it best to leave it there . . . 'Assuming one of us doesn't join the In Memoriam, God forbid.'

Wild life and flowers were our other interest in this remote region on the northern side of the Himalaya. How very different was the terrain to the lush lands of Nepal and India, where pine forests climb into the foothills and give way first to birch, rhododendron and juniper, and then to Alpine meadows where grow primulas, saxifrage, potentilla, iris and blue poppies – and many more Alpines. In those southern jungles there are bear, tiger and civet cats, while higher snow leopard hunt ibex, blue sheep and musk deer, hares, marmots and pika.

No spring flowers grew at the head of this barren valley. There were no trees for miles around. A few grasses were sprouting when we left in June. We saw blue sheep twice, and there were many hares around Rongbuk. Apart from a vole we were to meet and befriend later, birds were our only animal companions. A lonely Himalayan Griffon flew up and down the valley many times and Yellow Billed Choughs were common scavengers both at Base and up to 8000 metres. We saw around Base Tibetan Snow Finch, Hill Pigeon, Raven and a striking pale pink bird, the Great Rose Finch. Among the moraines Tibetan Snow Cock chuckled, while at Rongbuk we saw Tibetan Partridge, Guldenstadt's Redstart and Horned Lark.

We left Base again with the yaks and the five Tibetans on 10th April and wandered slowly up the East Rongbuk Valley. Adrian was clearly better acclimatised than on the previous trip: I felt terrible. Perhaps it was because of the Diamox I was using – usually a useful drug in the prevention of altitude sickness but which, in my case, had some unpleasant side effects. Ang Nuru, the leader of the yak herders, took my sack for the last hour. We camped at about five p.m. at the site of the prewar Camp 1 and the five Tibetans, being now the majority, looked after us. It is easy to be impatient with porters and yak herders on a march: living with them makes it easier to understand their ways. That afternoon they chipped the ice and boiled water on a yak dung fire, breaking bricks of tea and adding coarse salt. Dirty Tibetan bowls came out of grubby bags and were ladled gently full. A knob of yak butter is dropped into each bowl, smelling fatty and rancid. It floats on the surface and makes the Tibetan tea taste a little like a rotten, salty chicken soup: I almost grew to like it at the end. Ang Nuru motioned us into the make-shift shelter and fed us tea. There were ten or twelve pints between seven of us. He said the butter helps chapped lips. Then out came the meat. Raw leg of sheep, dried in the cold winds of the Tibetan plateau. They ripped slivers off the bones and chewed them, hard; we followed and once the art of eating raw lamb from a dirty sack had been accomplished the meat tasted quite good.

Two hours passed. The younger men gave buckwheat to the yaks, pounding up the grain with water into little cakes and mixing in a little coarse brown sugar. Ang Nuru brought out his prayer book and chanted for an hour, licking tsampa (roasted barley flour) from his bowl between verses. By nine, 'the meal' was being prepared. Wet tsampa was being rolled into little balls (incidentally cleaning the cook's hands in the process); the tsampa dumplings were thrown into the cauldron of water with fragments of sheep, salt and chilli – and boiled for an hour or so. We slipped off to bed by ten, before this feast was ready but, generous as ever, Ang Nuru woke us at eleven thirty with mugs of stew. We could not stomach the flavour but, trying hard not to upset our employee, we forced a little down before managing to pour the rest away. I feel I can eat almost anything but had to confess the tsampa stew had beaten me. The candles were out at twelve, the great yaks' eyes glinting in the moonlight, fearsome but harmless – perhaps the source of many a yeti scare. It was a cold night, – 13°C in the tent.

Dawn came with a grey glimmer around seven. The yak men struggled out of sheepskins, drew on their coarse wool trousers and jackets, socks and felt boots and were up, fetching ice and water, feeding their animals and checking their hoofs. The tea brewing ritual began again and, as before, we were looked after as part of the family. Tsampa, tasting faintly like dry Weetabix, is made into a paste with salt tea. This is the Tibetan breakfast cereal – how similar the carbohydrate breakfast is the world over.

We were off about nine. I was frightened of the falling stones above Camp 1½ and wanted to explore a safer route among the boulders of the frozen East Rongbuk stream. I spent an hour on thin ice slithering around – an unpleasant, longer, though safer alternative. We reached the walls of Changtse and the old Camp 2 by mid-afternoon, feeling energetic in a brilliant morning free of wind. The ritual of the previous night followed. It was bitterly cold, down to –26°C in the tent and, typically, the Tibetans had brought no extra clothing or sleeping bags, preferring to hoard the down gear we gave them rather than soil it. They snuggled together under sheepskins and emerged stiffly in the morning, grinning. They hurried and left early. Two yaks had already dropped off at Camp 1, four more were lame and I waited anxiously to see what would happen but I need not have worried. Three Tibetans picked up the yak loads, fully forty kilos apiece, and carried them themselves, arriving at Advance Base without complaint. They were good men.

We learnt much on that second yak carry. Our Tibetans were among the most friendly companions we'd ever had in the mountains: they cared about their animals and about us as if both were extensions of their families. Conversation was, however, a bit thin. Adrian speaks Nepali and they knew a few words learnt from traders. For the rest we had to learn Tibetan, soon mastering the words for spoon, mug, stew, yak, load and road. Merriment and obscenity were not far below the surface and this international language soon became part of the vocabulary, an unusual event in China where there is a strange prudishness about it all. We soon knew the Tibetan for farts and that Ang Nima had a very pretty sister.

Advance Base was empty when we arrived but the barren windswept rocks beside the glacier now seemed more friendly. The others had worked hard, building tent platforms and walls – the main mess tent was firmly anchored with rocks and ropes. The western sides of all the stones were blasted with frozen powder snow which had penetrated any opening in the tents and left a fine film of powder. It had clearly been windy. We looked across the glacier to the Ridge, rising like a huge dorsal fin from the bare ice. Two little figures were working hard on the Second Cave at about 7256 metres, and two more were higher on the Ridge. I felt impatient that things were not going faster and thought worriedly about when I said I would be home – we had already been away six weeks.

At six in the evening I talked to Joe on the radio. I am a pessimist about radio communication and seem to have had endless problems with radios on other expeditions. The tiny Sony sets which Joe had brought were already battered – they had been on two previous trips. It was a surprise to get through immediately and to hear that all was well. They would be down in two days.

Adrian and I settled down for our first night at 6400 metres. It was snowing slightly and the wind rising, roaring across the East Face of Changtse above us, crashing with explosive fury at the protruding rock buttresses. We heard the noise first like a distant peal of thunder, then the blast would sweep unchecked across the glacier, blowing a fine ice dust like powdered glass. A second explosion as it hit the tents, rattling the fabric with harsh, aggressive noise. The wind is never a friend here, it cannot serve us to fill our sails. My only use for it was to fly my kite at Base Camp.

The Advance Base mess tent was a gloomy dark green military box tent, battened down and reinforced with a rough stone table in the centre and food boxes, ropes, harnesses, cameras, books and radios scattered around. A smoked ham and salami hung from the roof, delicacies which we thought we might enjoy but which proved too rich for the inevitable loss of appetite which occurs above 5500 metres. Outside were more food boxes, fixed ropes and pitons, crates of film and boxes of personal gear beside each single tent. Each of our tents was so different, instantly recognisable, reflecting the personality of the owner. Joe's, Peter's and Adrian's were organised and tidy, Dick's spartan and half the size of any of the others. Chris's and mine were rather a mess.

The Choughs, yellow-billed black birds like crows, were our only companions, scavengers ready to eat anything. They seemed to nest – or at least to roost – in the rock turrets of the East Face of Changtse at 7000 metres, a windy spot for a home.

On our second evening, after a day spent organising loads, cooking and baking bread in a makeshift oven, it was less windy, even silent at times except for the pistol shots of the glacier as the ice groaned round the corner from the North Col. Suddenly there was a rustle within the tent, as if small stones were moving in the moraines beneath us. It continued and became more persistent and was obviously a creature. We waited excitedly to meet our unexpected companion and laid a trail of food away from the box beneath which the noise originated. We were soon rewarded when a pointed nosed brown rodent with a whiskered face popped up, saw us and vanished. 'Nibbles' was soon to become a firm friend. Probably a vole (a Sikkim Vole seems most likely) and clearly living permanently at 6500 metres – the site of these old camps – quite what he ate in the lean years I do not know. As the weeks passed we saw 'him' grow fat and become quite tame; he would come out when called to be fed and by the end of the expedition he had even found a mate. I suppose he originally came up in a load but, living there now permanently, we'd seen what was almost certainly the highest mammal on earth.

Chris returned on 14th April, alone and tired; the others were down by the evening. It was good to be together again and hear the news that work on the Second Snow Cave was advancing. They all looked exhausted but happy with the progress and I expected that we would all descend as planned to Base Camp the following day. There was, however, need to push out the route fast and they'd decided, perhaps unwisely, to rest at Advance Base for several days, rather than at Base, in order to save time. I thought they all picked at the food I prepared, even the fresh warm bread from the

6400-metre oven, rather than devouring everything edible like wolves.

'Deterioration' at high altitude due to persistent lack of oxygen occurs whenever man tries to live for long periods much above 5500 metres. Appetite falls off, sometimes dramatically. Sleep is fitful and one's energy gradually flags. Despite the relative comforts of Advance Base, plentiful food and enough warm clothing, it was perhaps an error to think that we could ever live there without our physical resources running slowly downhill. In retrospect I feel sure that the long periods spent above 6000 metres in the 1920s and 1930s, particularly with the terrain so disarmingly easy, contributed to the failure of the expeditions. Certainly later on this trip there was unanimous enthusiasm for resting at Base Camp, despite a twelve-mile walk.

Adrian and I left on 16th April to pick up the third and last yak carry. Pleased with ourselves we took six hours to get down and fell upon a large Chinese meal. Morale had improved. Mr Chen, the liaison officer, was back from Xegur, fit and well, and there was more mail from Lhasa.

We planned to rest and then return to Advance Base with the yaks and later attempt a peak of almost 7000 metres to the north. If we needed to justify what appeared to be a jaunt, our peak seemed to afford a remarkable view of the North East Ridge. We could also keep in radio contact.

It was not to be. We sensed something was wrong with the third yak carry early in the three-day journey. There was unnecessary argument about loads and we found that our five Tibetans had again brought no expedition clothing. As we left the prewar Camp 1, two of the yak herders stayed behind while the three who came said that they wanted to reach Advance Base that day instead of the next. We agreed. We had finished our journey by early afternoon, leaving ample time for the yak herders to drop back to reach prewar Camp 2 or, even at a stretch, Camp 1. No, they wanted to stay; yes, they'd like some whisky. We agreed.

Lom Sangu, the eldest Tibetan – and we were never good friends – eagerly grasped a bottle of White Horse and promptly drank it in one. His two companions huddled around the stove eating aspirins for their headaches, now quite unable to leave because Lom Sangu could not walk. Six hungry yaks shivered in the wind outside. They would leave at daybreak, about seven. We agreed. They could make us tea. We lent them a tent and sleeping bags which belonged to the absent climbers.

I had a fitful, headachey night, and pottered around after sunrise, brewing endless cups of tea. The Tibetans snored, two surfacing about nine, while one remained firmly inside the tent, coughing and groaning. We were irritated with them for they had outstayed their welcome. We were keen to get moving ourselves but could not leave them alone in the camp. In an effort to hurry them I poked my head inside their tent to glimpse an extraordinary scene. There was the entire expedition's rations of chocolate, several climbing ropes, tins, sweets, biscuits, adhesive tape, all being packed feverishly into Tibetan woollen bags by the man who was apparently sick.

My fury was uncontrolled. We hustled them out of the camp, having searched grubby folds of clothing and all their belongings. I felt cheated, hurt and intensely angry that our excellent relationship had been soured by this deception. We cancelled our plans for a peak, radio-ed the Ridge and set off after them to Base Camp. By nightfall on 21st April we were back at Base Camp. Mr Chen listened patiently to our problem with resignation born of many expeditions. Next day he harangued the Tibetans who seemed to apologise for their behaviour. We wished not to exact retribution but rather to make certain that they returned at the end of our stay to help us down with the loads. As usual on an expedition we were entirely dependent in some way upon the local people.

Three days later the others came down to rest.

8: Idle days

24th–28th April/Chris Bonington

It was a brilliant sunny morning at Advance Base on 24th April but the entire mountain was plastered with freshly fallen snow and we all felt we had made the right decision in coming down. There was a holiday atmosphere as we sorted out our gear and packed light sacks with exposed film to take back down to Base. I was the first away and I strode alone down the scoop of snow between the ice of the glacier and the rocky moraine. You can never relax completely above the snow line and suddenly I plunged downwards into a hidden crevasse. A momentary terror engulfed me but I came to a halt with my head just above the surface, my shoulders jammed between the narrow walls of ice. I, too, had been lucky; it had been just narrow enough for me to stop. Another fifteen centimetres wide and I could have gone all the way down.

Shaken and chastened, I struggled out and scuttled across to the rocks. It was harder walking, but at least they were safe. The others noticed the hole as they came down and were relieved to see my tracks emerging on the other side. Pete, plugged into the stereo sound of his little cassette player, felt good:

Walking down into oxygen always makes me feel strong. Locked into music the walk speeds past. It seems obvious now that we should have done this last time. I have eaten so little in the past three weeks. Full of thoughts and excitement as I go down, really a feeling of return. We haven't done badly up there, but we have been away such a long time; it is such a long time since I flew a kite at Xegur, even since we were last at Base Camp.

I purposefully blind myself to much of the beauty – our Ridge must be all that matters for a while.

Each landmark brought us closer to safety and comfort. The glimpse of the ice lake by the first camp that we had used on the way up and then, much closer, the tent we had left in place there, the cairn with the prayer flag that marked the junction with the Central Rongbuk Glacier, the sight of the spur at whose foot lay Base Camp and, at last, the stretch of flat shingle that led to the little tent village. There were so many tents for so few of us. Just the long walk across the flat and then Mr Chen and Mr Yu came out to greet me, warmly shaking my hand. Charlie and Adrian were down at the Rongbuk Monastery for the night. Then there was the big base tent with stacks of papers and magazines sent by David Mathew from Peking and cans of Budweiser beer brought in from Lhasa.

There were tiny new potatoes boiled in their jackets.

Half way through the afternoon there was a roar of a truck; we momentarily thought that this was Charlie coming back, but then there was the sound of American voices. We knew that the American Everest team were all up the Rongbuk Glacier. Could these be trekkers? We groaned at the thought, having no desire to make polite conversation, or to talk to lay people asking endless obvious questions. But we'd have to greet them. I ventured out of the tent, to be met by a vaguely familiar figure, big and slightly shambling with a long, rather battered face framed by a traditional Tibetan hat. It took a second or so for it to dawn on me. It was Jim Bridwell, the American climber who had stayed at our house a couple of years before. He was a legendary figure, with many new routes in Yosemite to his credit and, more recently, routes in Alaska and Patagonia. He had also climbed Cerro Torre, one of the steepest and most difficult rock peaks in the world, with a complete stranger, after his own companions had returned home.

After the first greetings, we found that Jim was part of a small expedition whose object was to ski around Everest. Leader and creator of the project was Ned Gillette, a well known cross-country skier who had been in the American Olympic team and had written one of the best handbooks on the sport before branching into expeditions, ski-ing across the Karakoram in 1980 and then ski-ing up and down Mustagh Ata in China the same year. He had with him his girlfriend, Jan Reynolds, also a strong competitive cross-country skier, and another skier, Rick Barker. Jim Bridwell was both climbing expert and film maker, and had led them up a new route on Pumo Ri the previous winter.

All this came out as we sat and talked and drank wine and beer around the table in the base tent. It was wonderful having fresh people to share our experience and friends to talk to. We reminisced, exchanged tales of mutual friends, swapped music cassettes and relaxed in a way that we had been unable to do for some weeks. The Americans were sponsored by Camel cigarettes, though Jim Bridwell was the only member of the team who smoked. They had made the Nepalese part of the trip the previous winter but had not been allowed to cross the frontier and were therefore now completing the Tibetan side, having flown in through Peking to Lhasa.

Ned was very much the organiser, in constant consultation with their liaison officer, juggling plans and possibilities in an effort to fix their trip from the Lho La, back down the West Rongbuk Glacier, up the East Rongbuk, over the Lhakpa La, which Mallory had crossed sixty years before and then into the Kangshung Valley by the Karpo La. It sounded an enjoyable, interesting trip, during which they would cover much exciting ground. In some ways I envied them, for they were doing something that was well within their powers, yet both Ned and Jim envied us and were already talking of plans to go to Everest, such is the lure of the highest point on earth. We spent the days relaxing at camp, sleeping much and eating well but also wondering about the immediate future.

Pete wrote in his diary:

As far as equipment, food and support (Charlie and Adrian) we couldn't have better. No expense or thought spared. Funny, despite all my hypochondria, I am going by far the best, am certainly the strongest of all those up there on the hill. For the first time, this was actually frustrating during this last go. But it is encouraging that the two steps were so very easy and so, possibly, the big towers and gendarmes are also going to be easier than we think.

But this mountain is so big, our project so vast, so long, that all our energies are consumed by it and have to be directed towards it. Even Chris has little left over for other things. I find books difficult to read, when on other trips I have always found reading to be a useful distraction. It is even difficult to concentrate on photography, as if it is an energy drain. And now other Everest books, other people's experiences on Everest – their dates, their efforts, their carries have a dwindling relevance as we build up our own experience of the mountain and the pattern of our own attempt becomes increasingly defined.

I learnt a lot on K2 in 1980. Before that I believed nothing could resist if I tried hard enough; but I do want so much to succeed this time. Kongur, in contrast, was playing. As Kissinger said to Nixon, 'A victor has a thousand relatives, but a loser is an orphan.'

And later that same day:

An idle morning drifting by; now listening to Fleetwood Mac, Bare Trees. Sort of weary, but not the same aches and pains, the same racking cough that I have up there on the Ridge; it is so difficult to be fully aware at altitude. Life inexorably becomes blinkered – 'Yes, I know I must eat, must force it down, must make a big effort each day' . . .

And yet we are a great compact little team, hardly a cross word ever between us. In a way, we all respect, sort of love each other, for we know that when the crunch comes each of us will do the right thing.

While Pete wrote, Dick worked on the swan he was carving. He had brought the mahogany with him and was slowly, patiently, chiselling out its gently curved neck. Joe either slept through the day or worked on the notes of his film, and I just slept and slept. That first night had developed into a spontaneous, happy party of talk and drinking, and stories that became increasingly maudlin, but I had not been able to stand the pace and had staggered early to bed, to lie listening to the steady beat of the stereo, awake yet too tired to join in.

The following day, 26th April, Charlie and Adrian returned from Rongbuk, relaxed and satisfied with their ascent of a minor peak. True, as we all gazed down the valley from Base Camp their 6200-metre

Digging the Third Snow Cave, Makalu on the skyline left

Our Third Snow Cave was the best one, complete with alcoves for cooking

Charlie contrived some makeshift inhalers to relieve
sore throats at Advance Base

left: Joe, Pete and Dick on the First Pinnacle

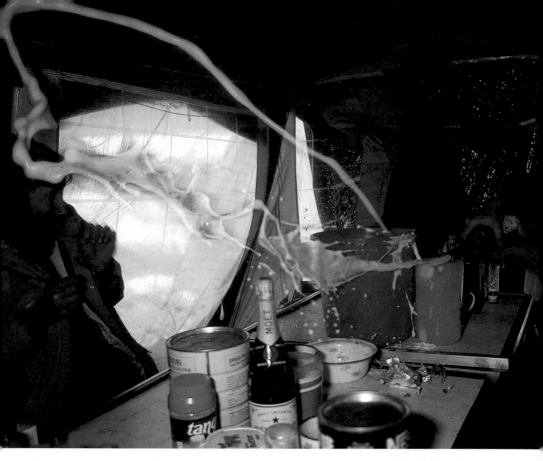

Looking east from the North Col

above left: The altitude proved too much for the champagne at Joe's thirty-fourth birthday party

left: Pete and Joe setting out on 15th May   *below:* Looking up from the North Col

First
pinnacle

Second
pinnacle

Final
pinnacle

NORTH RIDGE

✳ Joe and Pete last seen
1○ First possible spot they could come into sight
2○ They had to come into view here since there is a sheer cliff on the other side
☐ Orange tent sighted by Adrian
----- Possible route for them
⟶ Only feasible route past final pinnacle

Chris and Charlie searching the Kangshung Face

opposite: Pethangtse

Charlie carved a memorial to Pete and Joe which stands on a hillock near Base Camp

SUMMIT

SOUTH
COL

Final pinnacle
Second pinnacle
First pinnacle

Third snow cave

Second buttress
First buttress

Second snow cave

First snow cave

RAPHU LA

Final pinnacle

Second pinnacle

First pinnacle

High point 5 May

Third snow cave

ABOVE AND BELOW] *The Kangshung Face*
Route ——————— Fixed rope
* The point at which Pete and Joe were last seen from the other side
The most likely route they would have taken

summit did not look impressive. 'You mean that dramatic peak that domi-
nates the western side of the valley, to which the eye is drawn like a magnet?'
was the way Pete put it teasingly.

Charlie's diary:

*Adrian and I set off from Rongbuk, climbed a steep scree gully to the west and soon
look down on the monastery. After four hours we reach a crest, a fine line of shattered
rocks like a Lakeland ridge bare of snow. The weather looks appalling with tongues
of dense black cloud shooting down like sabres, pouring snow on to nearby hills.
There seems little point in staying on this bleak and windswept ridge at 6000 metres
but, having carried a tent here, we felt compelled to. We cook and settle down. The
idiot in me has brought a lightweight sleeping bag and I sleep little, shiver and feel
restless. Adrian snores peacefully as I wait for dawn.*

*It is clear. We look across to Nepal and from this unusual angle can see the three
ridges of Everest, the South East as a jagged silhouette and the West in profile as
well. Our peak is several hundred metres above us. By ten we are on the top bathed
in warm still sunlight. A delicate heave onto the tabletop of a rock pinnacle for a few
seconds' photography. 6200 metres on the altimeter and just over that on the map.
Away to the west the ranges of Gyanchung Kang and Cho Oyu, new and exciting
views. But Rongbuk was beckoning and we sped off down, down a steep scree
ridge, down through the rocks and across a stream in three hours.*

*Oh Rongbuk, the stream and the grass to lie on. How can anyone have thought
this is a barren, inhospitable place? It felt like Paradise that quiet afternoon as we
lay in the sun outside our tent. The monastery seems to have been destroyed with
unparalleled savagery. Not a room remains undamaged. We know little about its
remote past but Tilman, talking to the High Lama in 1938, concluded that it was
built in the early part of this century. There seems no way of telling but the
surrounding walls look reasonably new. The Chinese told us that its destruction took
place in 1969 and at that time the valley was uninhabited, except by the monks and
nuns – separated from each other only by forty minutes of trail.*

*The central hall is about eighteen by twenty-four metres and the surrounding walls
about 180 metres square. Many Mani stones and just a few terracotta clay
miniatures. And no efforts at restoration. The stupa outside the monastery is split in
two to ransack the relics within.*

*Recent visitors (which include many Europeans) appear to have decided that the
destruction of the building is inadequate – so they have used it as a rubbish dump and
lavatory, filling the place with tins, excrement and lavatory paper . . . we have a
long way to go to educate ourselves.*

*We stayed lazily on the river bank and talked to Chris at six p.m. on the radio.
They had come down to Base Camp from the Ridge for another rest. A truck drove
past. Some figures in red waved. We waved back. They looked rather smart,
macho, aggressive and flashy and I suppose they thought we were trekkers. We, of
course, felt rather superior!*

The next three days slipped away agreeably. We even had a picnic at the site
of the old British Base Camp. A picnic was something our Chinese staff found

difficult to understand, it being altogether too frivolous. Lying in the sun, the ubiquitous tape deck rolling, nibbling salami and Stilton, swilling red wine, it was easy to forget, at least for a short time, the presence of Everest towering there at the head of the valley. It was concealed by the low moraine ridge on which had once stood the memorial to Mallory and Irvine.

'Pass those nuts over, please.'

'More pâté?'

'Want some more wine?'

'I'll borrow *Flesh Wounds* when you've finished it, if I may.'

Charlie flew his kite with the exuberance of a small boy. A Lamergeyer circled overhead. Conversation became blurred as I dropped off into a doze. I could be lying on the grass in the Lakes during a family picnic. Dimly I longed for the end of the expedition, longed to be home, to see my Lakeland hills and walk up High Pike, to get out rock climbing with the lads on the long summer evenings.

The three days' rest were nearly over. It was 28th April. Charlie and Adrian walked up to prewar Camp 1 that afternoon. We were to follow the next morning, walking straight through to Advance Base in the day. Time was galloping past all too quickly. April had all but gone and we still had not reached the Pinnacles – but at least the weather was getting kinder. The ice lake beside Base Camp was beginning to break up; each day the stream ran higher. It was even possible to wander around the camp in shorts and a T-shirt during the middle of the day. Surely the Ridge would be kinder to us than last time?

9: *The third foray*

29th April–7th May/Chris Bonington

The holidays were over. On 29th April Pete, plugged into his cassette, was away first: 'I'm listening to classical for the walk up. It's less imposing than pop music and I can choose my own rhythm . . . I've at least had some reasonable food; fried eggs inside my tum, Mars bars in my little sack to keep me going on this long walk; I feel fit, though light.'

Dick was close behind, but, Pete was determined to keep his own pace, and quietly strode on to the music of Mahler's Resurrection Symphony. On the way up, each of us tended to walk in his own little world. Joe had set out last of all, but overtook me before the junction of the East Rongbuk Glacier. I plodded up slowly, following the trail of scattered yak dung, the abandoned telephone wires of previous expeditions and the occasional daubs of Japanese red paint.

It was noticeable how a tenuous path had formed in the few weeks of use. The journey to Advance Base which originally had taken three days was now just a matter of hours. Dick took a mere six hours, I a more modest nine. Next morning we packed polythene bags full of food and Gaz cylinders and set off for the Ridge. Charlie and Adrian were going to accompany us as far as the foot of it, carrying the big 16mm cine camera so that Joe could get some good close-up action shots. It was typical of the thought and work he put into the filming. He had already spent some time with Charlie and Adrian, briefing them both on the working of the camera and also basic film techniques.

It was a savage return to the mountain. The wind blasted across the Raphu La, sweeping the fresh snow from the Ridge and giving us perfect cramponing conditions, but it was so strong that in the worst gusts we had to stop, crouched, clinging to our ice axes. I could not help feeling discouraged, for I seemed to have gained no benefit at all from our rest. Pete commented:

Chris walks very slowly, resting it seems at every step, and eventually not far from the 'schrund, the others overtake us. 'Does Chris always go so slow?' whispers Adrian . . .

I'm worried about being 'type cast' as always climbing and cooking with Chris and have made little hints to Dick and Joe. But it's not up to me to suggest, 'cos I don't want to hurt CB. Chris arrives late and says he feels he's hardly had a rest at all – he does get depressed easily. But he does bounce back and says, 'It's my turn to cook, you did it last time.' I'd forgotten.

This was a feeling I was never made aware of. Although I had doubts about my own ability to get to the top, I never had any about the others. I was convinced we had a good chance of success. On my good days I dreamed of getting there myself and on the bad ones wondered at what stage I might have to drop back to a purely supporting role.

The following day, 1st May, was an easy one. It took barely two and a half hours to reach the Second Snow Cave. This time it was to be the turn of Pete and me to sleep near the entrance and, since I had cooked the previous night, Pete had the unenviable spot on the outside, though with the snow-proof door it was less of a hardship. We had the entire afternoon to cook, read and discuss our plans for the next few days. We had settled on my proposal to move one pair straight up to the top of the shoulder at 7850 metres, and for them to camp if necessary while they dug the cave. The other pair would drop back to the Second Snow Cave and rejoin them the following day.

Pete commented: 'I'm agitated about how the teams will be split up; very agitated but not so much that I dare risk saying anything and being misunderstood. So I trust that Providence will guide us – and we draw bits of paper for the next couple of days' sportsplan.'

Pete's prayers were answered. He and Dick were to stay on the shoulder, while Joe and I did the second carry.

'Well, I'm glad, anyway,' said Joe, 'at least it'll give me another night sleeping at a lower altitude.'

We let the afternoon slip away, even though there was a lot to do, for we had all the food to sort out and pack. It was Dick who had the innate self-discipline to urge us into action. We sorted out five days' food and fuel, leaving behind much of the freeze-dried meat, which we all found unpalatable. Our standard diet had become a handful of muesli in the morning and cheesy mashed potato at night. We divided the food into two poly bags for Joe and me to carry the next day.

In the morning, as usual I got away first. We had brought with us a length of rope to leave across the easy-angled slabs leading to the snow slope of the First Buttress, but now clear of snow, it was once again straightforward and anyway there was nowhere to anchor the rope, so it was left at the far end in case we should ever need it.

Pete caught up with me at the top of the First Buttress and he and Dick moved steadily together towards the second length of fixed rope. Joe had been filming, but he also passed me. I was determined not to let them get too far ahead, and stayed doggedly behind them.

Pete had now pulled away from the rest of us:

Wonder how long it will be to the top of this long-sought landmark? Can we really just traverse around it to the col on the other side? It looks no worse than the sort of ground we have been traversing for miles down below . . . but soon I'm out of sight of the others, solo-ing with a lot of pauses for gasps, across an intricate bit of

ground, across steep slopes only tenuously attached, it seems, to the rock of the
mountainside, over little steps, round bulges, picking out a line traversing about
thirty to sixty metres below the crest of the ridge.

By this time the afternoon cloud had rolled in, filling the great bowl of the
Kangshung Face and overflowing on to our side of the Ridge in breakers
that enveloped us and then dissipated in the tearing wind. It was like the
incoming tide, getting imperceptibly deeper until each one of us was
enclosed in a world of driving snow. Pete had disappeared from sight
around a corner. Joe and Dick were just ahead, Dick having difficulty on a
steep little overlapping wall that barred the way. To avoid it, I took a
slightly higher line and as a result overtook him. This is how Dick felt: 'As
the others pulled away I gave up the struggle to keep up. Bugger it, I'll go at
my own pace and forget the unspoken recriminations. I put it down to an off
day. Funny how you feel bad about it, as though you're not pulling your
weight.'

The steps made by Pete and Joe were vanishing under the fresh snow as
Dick and I stumbled up over snow-covered rocks probing our way through
the mist. Out in front, Pete was thrusting forward on to new ground:

At last I can see round the corner, into the col, the rest of the Ridge looming
through the clouds towards the Pinnacles and what now appears as a prominent
inset gully, plunging down towards the glacier . . . No, it's steep round the
corner, and I climb straight up. There is no way we can avoid going round the top
of this summit. Also there is the spur running up from the Kangshung side. It gives
us our only hope for a snow cave. We can't afford to pour all that effort we did last
time into hacking a cave out of ice and rock.

Some rocks, a snowy plateau; I dump my sack and feel a different person –
what a difference without that unwelcome weight, to be able to move about.
No-one has been up here before and I can breathe and look around. There must be
a cornice somewhere. I walk near the rocks, down a few feet to the col on the other
side. Good, quite safe, we can walk to the foot of the steep part where we'll have to
fix ropes at the start of the Pinnacles.

I come back and Joe arrives. I uncoil a rope and he belays me as I peer over the
east side. By a stroke of luck I find the top of the spur coming up the other side,
although there is no indication along the edge to tell where it could be. Enthused, I
kick down it. Below the slope goes down quite steeply and then broadens into a
shoulder. I get the shovel and dig a bit, yell back up that it should be fantastic for
snow caving.

Joe has a long way to go back down and leaves. As I start shovelling he points
out that I'm a bit near the cornice that runs into the main ridge from this subsidiary
spur but says, 'It should be OK.'

I reached the top of the shoulder at 7850 metres just as Joe was about to
start down, dumped my bag full of food and Gaz cylinders, and peered over
the edge to see Pete's boots sticking out of the slope. He had burrowed the

entrance passage to the cave. I wished him the best of luck and started back down, to pass Dick a short way below the crest. The tracks were now completely covered and the visibility so bad, that I gave him explicit instructions on the route so that he would be sure of finding the cave. He was going very slowly and was obviously tired. When Dick reached the top of the shoulder, he also noticed how close to the cornice was the hole that Pete had started. He suggested putting up the tent, but Pete hated the idea of leaving the relative shelter of the lee side of the Ridge. 'It's so windy on the Ridge, and here, just a few feet down, it's so warm and quiet and the snow is so good.'

Dick reluctantly agreed they should dig on but complained, 'I don't know what happened on the way up; I just ran out of steam above the top of the Buttresses.'

He started to dig, but became increasingly worried by the proximity of the cornice and persuaded Pete to have a careful look. They decided to abandon excavation for the night and pitch a tent on top of the shoulder. Pete dug out a rectangular depression in the snow in which to sink the tent, as some protection from the driving wind.

Damn, it's so cold and I forgot to tie on the guy lines to the outer skin of the tent. I have to shelter inside and tie the loops and then go outside and tie them onto the tent loops with freezing fingers, anchoring the tent walls with everything I can stick into the snow – poles, hammers, axes, anything that will stay. I'm determined that we shouldn't take off. Dick goes straight inside and doesn't budge again.

It's not very pleasant inside, with the snow and ropes weighing down the valance and the tent flapping madly in the wind . . . Prop the stove precariously in the middle – a couple of spills, but we manage to eat a couple of packets of noodles each.

While Pete and Dick were getting installed for the night, Joe and I dropped back to the Second Snow Cave. Joe quickly vanished from my sight and I went down on my own, the footprints already covered in fresh snow. The occasional marker wand and our two lengths of fixed rope were the only reminders that anyone had ever been here before. I had reached that level of weariness, when even in descent, I needed to stop for a rest every few yards. How long could I go on pushing myself to this degree? Could I make it back up to the top of the shoulder tomorrow, and after that, the Pinnacles? Could I keep going at over 8000 metres? I was now at the top of the First Buttress. Come on, concentrate on the ropes, clip in correctly. I slid and stumbled down, left my harness and ascendeurs clipped to the rope at the bottom, and carefully front-pointed down the final stretch. I go so much more nervously when exhausted. I teetered across the snow-covered slabs, crampon points scraping ineffectively on the smooth rock and was grateful for the final easy slopes leading to the snow hole.

Joe was already in his sleeping bag, the stove in the corner purring quietly, heating water for a brew. I slumped on to my mat and just could not stop myself crying. They were tears of exhaustion, of frustration, of despair at my own weakness. Joe didn't say anything, just quietly let me get over it, and then offered me a brew. I muttered apologies but he sympathetically dismissed them, saying I'd feel better in the morning. That night he did the cooking, but I raised the energy to crawl out of the cave to make the evening radio call. We could hardly hear Pete up on the shoulder, for there was too much mountain between us, but Charlie was very clear. He and Adrian were off on another climb. They had crossed the East Rongbuk Glacier and were camped near Kartaphu, beneath a peak of almost 7000 metres, which they hoped to climb the next day. They could see us clearly and had a fine view of the entire North East Ridge. After the usual queries about the progress of the Falkland Islands war, Charlie was able to relay messages from Pete, asking us to pick up all the gear dumped at various spots on the way up.

After a good night's sleep in our now roomy cave, my resolve returned, and I was the first away, carrying my personal gear and a few items of climbing equipment that were still to go up. Joe soon caught up with me and, on the slopes above the Second Buttress, he chose a slightly different route from mine and began to pull away. Soon my progress had slowed to a crawl but at last I reached the crest and flopped down for a rest. Gradually it pervaded my consciousness that someone was below me and I glanced back to see Joe coming up behind. He had reached the top about an hour before and, realising that I was having a struggle, had decided to come back to help me with my rucksack on the final stretch. Unfortunately, because of the slight difference in our routes, he'd missed me. It was too late to let him carry my sack but I felt immensely touched by his kindness. Going back to help someone at that altitude shows a very real concern. We plodded slowly those last few metres up over the rounded snow dome and there below us on the other side of the Ridge, was a ledge carved out of the snow and the gaping hole dug by Dick and Pete during the day. It was a superb snow cave. The snow was just the right consistency, firm, but not too hard. The chamber had an alcove at either end for the cooking stove, it was easy to scoop out snow for making our brews and, being on the lee side of the Ridge, was sheltered from spindrift.

Joe and I were cooking at one end, Pete and Dick at the other. As so often happened, once all four of us were squeezed in, the cave was barely big enough. We discussed what to do next day and decided that Dick should drop back down to the top of the Second Buttress where we had left some ropes, bring them back up and then enlarge the hole, while the three of us should go to the foot of the Pinnacles and start climbing them.

Next morning dawned fine. The Kangshung Face dropped beneath us in a huge concave bowl. We could see the South Col on the other side of the summit at about the same height as ourselves. From there it was a mere five or six hours to the summit. We, on the other hand, were nearly two miles

from the summit, with the jagged Pinnacles between us and the comparatively easy ground of the upper part of the Ridge. We could now see the top
clearly but this seemed remote, dwarfed by the immediate threat of the
Pinnacles. The Ridge curved gently and easily to the foot of the first one, a
triangle of snow-veined rock, leading to a shapely point.

Pete was first away from the cave, striding steadily over the crisp snow,
keeping a few feet below the corniced crest. Joe and I followed, carrying
some ropes and pitons. Pete reached the foot of the First Pinnacle in about
two hours. Joe and I were three-quarters of an hour behind him. I
scrambled out in front, clambered up a small rock wall and looked round for
a belay. The rock was hard, black and slaty, with very few cracks. There
was nowhere for a piton belay, but there was a huge block iced into the
slope, and I draped the rope round the top of this. Pete was obviously raring
to get at the Pinnacle, so Joe and I tossed for who should hold his rope. I won
so Joe set off back to the cave to get a brew on.

Pete started up the bottom snow slope of the Pinnacle. This led up to a
rocky buttress, split by a shallow ice groove at about thirty metres. He
hunted around for a crack in which to hammer in a piton anchor, but they
were all blind, so he had no choice but to continue up the groove, bridging
out on sloping rock holds on either side, looking constantly for a suitable
crack. The time crept by and I stamped and shivered, watching Joe wander
back along the ridge. The rope crept out through my fingers. It was nearly at
an end. No alternative but to tie on another rope. Had Pete slipped, nothing
could have saved him and he'd probably pull me off as well.

A deeper ringing tone echoed down. He had at last got in a decent peg,
but he didn't stop there. Obviously it was not a good stance. Another couple
of pitons and he reached some broken ledges and hammered in a final
anchor. It had taken nearly three hours. Cold and shivery, I followed, trying
to put as little weight as possible on the rope. It had been a fine lead and one
that Pete had enjoyed. As I followed, jumaring up the rope, he carried on,
unbelayed but towing a rope behind him. I joined him when he paused. He
now moved diagonally over quite easy ground and ran out another thirty
metres. I set off, hammering in an intermediate anchor to make the rope
easier to follow. This at last was real climbing. By the time I reached Pete
the cloud had closed in and it was beginning to snow but he was determined
to reach a little notch in the Ridge about thirty metres above.

*And the straight-up pitch is great fun – solid rock; don't put in a runner for a
while, in case Chris has to attach another rope; eventually I reach the Ridge.
Great, it's firm. I can sit astride it, uncomfortable but safe. Snow softish on the
other side. Rocks near, but crackless. Can I climb higher? Seems OK. The next
bit doesn't look too steep. That was my objective for today, but time is running
out. It's around six thirty.*

*Chris yells up asking me to decide what I'm doing. He's getting cold. My hands
were intensely cold down there, but now with the grip and the climbing,*

everything's warmed up . . . I put two deadmen in, one on the Ridge, the other through the cornice of the Ridge and start off down; scrape around and get a kingpin in; good, need the deadman higher up. I then abseil, using full body harness.

Put out a lot of effort today and feel very, very weary. It is misty and snowy and even Joe's tracks have disappeared and I can only follow Chris for a short distance. I'm staggering with fatigue, particularly when I have to go uphill for that little bit to the top of the shoulder and can see Chris through the cloud arriving spectacularly at the Snow Cave. Big relief to arrive there myself.

Joe records our encouraging comments and coughs. So much coughing; I've never coughed or retched so much before in my life. Where does the mucus come from? It's because we're in the Death Zone or the 'regrettable' zone, as Joe calls it. When cells are dying the phlegm comes, to move it on and out.

Dick, bless him, has a brew ready. I'm even going off tea at altitude, but liquid always revives and slowly we settle to almost normal and can face the thought of a little food . . . Chris can't stand the smell of milk powder and retched twice at the entrance. Dick has had peas and rice prepared for a long time and I spoon it painfully down until it becomes cold and impossible.

We're going back up tomorrow. I'm sure this sort of thing hasn't been done before at such an altitude, but I think this is the only way at the moment to progress, for two people to think, 'This is my day, my responsibility.' We must get going early and go all out and do our maximum in this time.

It was to be the turn of Dick and Joe next morning, while Pete and I took it easy, having a leisured breakfast and then following them with a load of ropes and tents. By the time we had emerged from the snow hole, they were only half way across the easy stretch leading to the Pinnacles. Fresh snow had fallen during the night but they were also tired and moving slowly. Dick had now been up here at 7850 metres for three nights, Joe two. As soon as we set off Pete pulled ahead, reaching the foot of the Pinnacles by the time I was half way across, while Dick, followed by Joe, was moving very slowly up the fixed rope. They were going no faster than we had the previous day when we had pushed the route out for the first time. It was the insidious effect of altitude, the gradual slowing up caused by sleeping at nearly 8000 metres without any oxygen. Plodding in their wake, I certainly felt it. At last I reached the foot of the Pinnacles but could not face the prospect of that long slow toil up the fixed ropes. Hardly thinking, I dumped the tent and ropes on the boulder at its foot, and, racked with guilt, fled back down the Ridge. At least I could have a meal ready for them when they returned. Dick had now reached the high point and sorted out the ropes and climbing gear, while Joe came up the final rope length. The Ridge jutted steeply above them, looking threatening, even dangerous. The day had started fine but a scum of high grey cloud now blanked out the sun and the very flatness of the light increased the feeling of threat.

Since Dick was first at the high point, and had therefore had the longest rest, it was his pitch:

I hope that Joe will offer to take this pitch as I've been in front up to now. I can't ask him but I console myself with the fact that the pitch after will be his lead. Personal survival; it's hard to think beyond oneself. This self-absorbed suffering must be a cardinal sin.

I select my gear – we are short of dead men. Hopefully, I take some ice screws. Joe is encouraging and we decide on a system of communication. I set off, wary. The steepness becomes alarming. I thrust in both tools. There's a crusty layer which gives a false sense of security, but soon that disappears and I'm left floundering. The trick is to kick a step that will not collapse into the lower one. I sink both arms deep into the snow; gaining little height but quite a lot of horizontal ground and I'm feeling the lack of protection. It's going to be a monster swing if the snow collapses. I become increasingly aware that I might be on a corniced ridge that could collapse. It's a frightening pitch and I have to fight hard.

But the angle began to relent and the snow became firmer. Dick had run out the full length of rope. By this time Pete had caught up with Joe and from the shoulder I could watch their slow progress, three tiny dots clinging to the corniced ridge.

Pete wondered:

The surface crust sounds, and is, hollow and underneath it is deep, collapsing and insubstantial. Why didn't Dick even squeal, 'Hey, watch me, Joe, this is really unstable and dangerous'? A very cool lead and I (as Joe did) find even following it up a rope very frightening.

When Dick reached the end of the rope, he managed to find a placement for a deadman, and called down to Joe: 'It's safe, you can come up now.'

He was able to sit down and rest while Joe jumared up the fixed rope. On arrival Joe immediately started to set up the cine camera while Dick sorted out the belay so that he could safeguard Joe for the next rope length. The angle looked easier and the Ridge had broadened, giving the promise of firmer snow. It was while doing this that Dick became aware of a strange sensation of numbness spreading down his left arm and leg. At first he thought it was just the cold, but then his left cheek and even the left side of his tongue became numb. He bit it, and there was no feeling and yet when he bit the right side it felt normal.

'There's something funny going on with me, Joe,' he said.

'What is it?'

And Dick described the symptoms.

'You'd better go down. Pete can belay me on this pitch. There's no point three of us being up here.'

As Dick waited for Pete to come up the rope, he couldn't help remembering the story of Art Gilkey, the American climber who had had a thrombosis in his leg high on K2 in 1953. They had been trapped by a storm at their top camp and when it ended his five team mates had tried to evacuate him, lowering and hauling him down the steep slopes. They had had one narrow escape when one of them slipped, pulling off the others, to be saved by the belay of their anchor man. It was shortly after this that Gilkey somehow slipped out of his harness and fell to his death. It seems quite possible that he did this on purpose, realising that the others would almost certainly lose their lives if they continued their attempt to save him. These were Dick's thoughts as he huddled on the crest. Once Pete arrived he could start down. By the time he got back to the snow cave he felt perfectly normal, even a little shame-faced at having made a fuss and having to come back early.

At the high point Joe, belayed by Pete, had started up the next stretch of the Ridge. The snow had now improved and he was able to make good steady progress, kicking methodically into the snow just below the crest. Another fifty metres of rope and he slotted in a deadman to bring up Pete. Just two pitches that day. They were still sixty metres short of the top of the First Pinnacle; they dumped the ropes and the tent Pete had carried up and started down.

Back at the Third Snow Cave, I had started melting snow for brews, when Dick crawled in. Diffidently he described what had happened to him, saying that he felt perfectly all right again. He was also worried about frostbite.

'Does my nose look funny?' he asked.

'It's a bit purple. Let me feel it.'

It was warm to the touch, not cold and frozen.

'It'll be all right. I think you've just had a nip.'

I was puzzled, a little worried about the other symptoms, but had no idea what they could be and anyway was preoccupied by my own fatigue. Joe and Pete got back about an hour later, tired, but elated with the progress they had made.

I had started a large panful of cheesy potato, by now our staple food. By the time they had brushed the snow from their down suits and boots and had crawled into their sleeping bags it was ready. I lifted it off the stove by its handle to pass it over Joe, who was next to me, for Pete to have the first spoonful. As I lifted it above Joe, the handle gave way, and the pan toppled into his sleeping bag, covering it in a gelatinous yellow goo – Oh shades of Kongur! I'd spilled boeuf Stroganoff all over him on that expedition; but this was worse, for it was like glue, clinging greasily to both our sleeping bags and setting in the cold.

Joe, ever self-controlled, said nothing at all, just lay back and left me to spoon up the fast-freezing mess. I scraped it back into the pan and eventually recovered about a quarter of it, which I reheated, but somehow we had lost our appetites. Pete, however, cooked a rival meal for himself and Dick. That night we did not talk much about plans for the next morning. I think we were all too tired. I had been in favour of going back down for a rest, feeling that we were now exhausting ourselves just getting up to the high point and then, as had happened that day, only pushing out two rope lengths. Pete and Dick, however, felt that we must, at all costs, get the route run out further along the Pinnacles to be sure of crossing them and making an effective bid for the summit on our return.

It was only next morning, 6th May, after a couple of brews and a half cup full of muesli, that we discussed seriously what to do next. It was ten o'clock before we finally came to the decision to descend. I left my sleeping bag, all my spare clothes and some camera equipment in the cave. It was a form of demonstration to myself that I was going to return, that I would not give up, though in the back of my mind there were now some very serious doubts.

The slopes below were covered with nearly half a metre of fresh snow, making the descent slow and insecure. Even so we climbed unroped, picking a way down slowly. Back at the Second Snow Cave we paused for a few minutes. We were late for the mid-day call that we had arranged, but after several attempts managed to raise Charlie. It was good to make contact and we told him that we'd be back down at about six o'clock that evening.

Then we set off once more, Dick first, me just behind. He stopped half way down the long easy slope towards the top of the spur at Point 7090 and I quickly caught him up. His crampon had fallen off and he was struggling to push it back on. I crouched in the snow beside him, tried to give him a hand and, holding the crampon, thrust it up against the sole of his overboot. Dick toppled off balance, grabbed me, and pulled me over as well. We rolled over, did a somersault in the soft snow, both clawing at its surface to stop ourselves. What a stupid lunatic way to go, but we came to a stop, laughing nervously. I apologised for my over-eagerness and Dick, struggling with his crampon without further help from me, eventually jammed it back on his boot. We continued down, roping up over the steep slopes immediately above the First Snow Cave, moving now even more cautiously, until at last we could relax at the crest of the arête leading down to the glacier. Even this though, required care. There was a very real danger of avalanche as we picked our way down it. Once back on the glacier we roped up and plodded back towards Advance Base.

Pete wrote:

And what a weary little gang we must look as we topple across – call them mountaineers? They can't even walk across the horizontal! Such a close relationship between us all on this trip; a closely knit group of mates.

Joe, dedicated as ever to the film, had instructed Charlie and Adrian to come out and film our return. Charlie commented in his diary:

And so they're back, shortly after six p.m., captured on celluloid by Adrian and me as budding cameramen. Oh, they came up that slope so slowly. At first we thought something had happened to them because we could see their tracks coming down from the Raphu La into a piece of dead ground and then we waited and waited and waited. The answer was quite clear; they were exhausted and crept in like old men, but rallied a bit, like soldiers, for the last few yards to Advance Base – which is exactly what we didn't want on the film!

We sat outside the big greenie tent and told Charlie what had happened, particularly, what had happened to Dick. He asked briefly about symptoms but was non-committal, murmuring that he'd have a look at Dick back at Base Camp. And there were all the good things of Advance Base, fresh bread and a fresh vegetable broth that slid down deliciously after our almost inedible dehydrated foods of the mountain.

We all had sore throats and that night Charlie made for us his own brand of inhaler, bashing a hole in the lid of a mess tin and pushing through it a length of rubber tubing so that we could breathe in the steam from a brew of honey, lemon and whisky. We looked like a group of opium smokers crouched round the stone table in the middle of the mess tent, as we coughed and hawked and spoke of our adventures of the previous days. Adrian and Charlie told us of the latest exploits of our mascot 'Nibbles' and of how he was growing ever fatter on his rich diet. Whatever would he do when we left?

Observing us, Charlie commented in his diary:

All are fucked, sore-throated and so on, but well. Dick had a strange turn yesterday. Numb left face, left tongue, left arm for five or ten minutes while on the climb. No headache or visual disturbance. I haven't examined him, other than his eyes, where he has florid papilloedema[1] with haemorrhages and ghastly dilated veins. The diagnosis is easy – a small stroke. What's to be done now?

Chris seems quiet, much quieter than usual and I put this down to tiredness. Peter is, I think, very pent up without much to show for it and his 'act' of being helpless palls a bit. He seems to have less fun in him than before but I think this is merely the state of the climb.

Joe, however, seems an easier person this time, possibly because he and filming fit in well together – I think this will be a superb film. Perhaps because we have to help him very specifically, like walking over to the bergschrund and doing some cramponing in that foul gale – he turns round and is helpful back in turn. I find, in fact, that having been more cross with Joe in the distant past, I do feel very much more warm to him than I used to be.

After a lazy morning we set off at around two o'clock, just after Jan Reynolds and Rick Barker of the American ski team arrived with their yak herders. They were planning to use our camp for a few days before completing their circumnavigation of Everest. We chatted for a short time and then went our different ways.

[1] Swelling of the optic nerve in the retina – a problem which occurs occasionally at extreme altitude.

On the way down Charlie told me that he was sure that Dick had had a stroke and that it was most unlikely he would be able to go back on to the Ridge. And what about me, I wondered? Had I the strength to make it to the summit or, for that matter, could I keep up with Pete and Joe?

The sun had a real warmth and everywhere we could hear the sound of running water. The summer had arrived and conditions seemed perfect but had we the strength to return, to climb the Pinnacles and then go for the summit?

10: Everything is changed

7th–12th May/Chris Bonington

As I walked slowly into Base Camp, our Chinese staff came out to greet me, shaking me warmly by the hand. Joe and Pete were in the base tent, reading their mail. For a few moments Everest was forgotten as I skimmed through my letters, digging out first the ones from Wendy, so that I could transport myself back to our Lakeland home and fells, then letters from the children and from friends. There were cans of beer, a thermos full of hot water for tea and a bowl full of delicious new potatoes.

Charlie was with Dick, examining him. We were subdued in spite of our pleasure at being back in the comparative warmth and luxury of Base. We were all waiting for Charlie's verdict but instinctively avoided talking about it, turning, once we had read our letters, to the old newspapers and magazines that David Mathew had sent us. For once the cassette recorder had been left off. All you could hear was the gurgle of running water, the rustling of the wind and the chatter of our Chinese staff. The atmosphere was charged with foreboding, but I did not want to rush into any rash decisions which we might regret later, and therefore suggested that we waited till the morning before we discussed anything.

Charlie completed the examination of Dick in his tent, told him that he had had a mild stroke and that he would have to consider seriously whether or not he should return to altitude. Dick did not sleep much that night as he tried to determine what he should do. He had felt wonderfully fit on the way down from Advance Base. As usual he had arrived back about half an hour in front of anyone else. He desperately wanted to go on with the expedition, both to share in the work of the team and to fulfil his personal ambitions. He seemed to have absolute confidence in his own and the team's ability to complete the climb and passionately wanted to be part of this. Charlie had left him with the onus of making the decision and at first Dick resolved to carry on with the climb, convincing himself that the stroke had only been a very minor one and that he was now fully recovered.

Charlie had very little sleep that night either, for he was worried that he had not spelt out sufficiently clearly the seriousness of what had happened to Dick. He was up early the following morning and went over to Dick's tent.

'I've been thinking it over, Dick. I'm afraid I've got to tell you not to go back up again. You've got to think of what would happen if you did have another stroke. If you were paralysed, it wouldn't just be your life at risk, it'd be the others as well, because they'd have to get you down. I'm sorry.'

'How likely is it to happen again?'

'It's difficult to say. But it is a distinct possibility. I don't think it's a risk you're justified in taking, if only for the sake of the others.'

Dick was silent for a long time. There were so many implications. Would he ever be able to return to the high peaks of the Himalaya? How could he adjust to a life without mountaineering? He then agreed with Charlie that this was the only possible course.

Later on that day, Charlie recorded:

It's strange how at altitude, or in the heat of the moment, it's difficult to make obvious decisions. At Base Camp I had a good look at Dick and superficially he was perfectly well, admitting to, rather than complaining of, his left hand feeling somewhat 'thick' – no more.

There were, however, definite signs of his stroke when I examined him. The implications are heavy:

Descent to sea level is the only way to sort this out properly, and messing around here at Base is unacceptable.

He really should have a medical escort, but I don't see how I can leave the rest of the team without medical cover.

The question of his return in future years is knotty. In his place, I wouldn't go above 6,000 metres, particularly as he has had what sounds like papilloedema several years ago at very high altitude.

It was with a heavy heart that I decided all this and told him, but he does understand. Thank God we didn't have a paralysed man on our hands. This is all that can be said.

Charlie suggested to Dick that it might be easier for him if he went for a walk after breakfast while the rest of us were told and decided what to do. Charlie's voice slipped into that unemotional, slightly clinical tone of all doctors as he explained the position. It was something that we had expected but nonetheless the formal acknowledgement of the inevitable was still grim. This also seemed the right time to tell them of a decision I'd just made myself. We could at least then discuss how we were going to cope with this new set of circumstances.

'I'm afraid I've got yet another bombshell,' I told them. 'I've been thinking about it ever since we got back down to Base Camp and, the more I go into it, the more I realise I just can't keep up with Joe and Pete. Quite honestly I'm not at all sure I could even get back up to our high point.'

'Don't you think you'll be all right after a few days' rest?' said Pete. 'You know, we're all shattered at the moment. I don't think any of us should make any decisions for the time being.'

'But I really have thought this out, and I think we do need to start thinking of what we are going to do. I'm not going to change my mind on this one. You know we've always thought it'd be useful to have a line of retreat down to the North Col, but we've just never had the time or energy to go there. If Charlie, Adrian and I establish a camp on the North Col, you and Joe could drop down the North Ridge once you've climbed the Pinnacles – either after getting to the top or, if you take too long getting over the Pinnacles, you could come straight down to the Col, have a rest and then go back again. You never know, I might even have rested enough to go with you.'

'That's a lot to take in at the moment,' said Joe. 'I agree with Pete. We shouldn't make any decisions in a hurry.'

'You know, Chris, all our recent trips have been hard work like this,' said Pete. 'We're not supermen. We're probably just as tired as you are.'

'You've no bloody idea how much I've been pushing myself!' I exploded, almost tearful in the violence of my own sense of doubt and emotion. 'I've never pushed myself so hard, never felt so out of control. I'm sorry. I know my own limits and I've reached them.'

The conversation waxed and waned. Pete apologised for being flippant and I said I realised he didn't really mean it. It was half way through the morning when Dick came into the tent. He had shaved off his beard, it was as if he was already in a different world. We all stopped talking. What could one possibly say. I just muttered:

'We're terribly sorry, Dick.'

He could not hold back his tears. It was not only Everest, or a matter of leaving the close companionship of our little group, it was his entire life that was altered. Dick was not interested in fame or money but he loved the mountains, needed to stretch himself to his own limits – and now, all that seemed closed to him. But he quickly got hold of himself.

'I'll be all right. It's just getting used to it that's difficult.'

We talked around it and then I asked him whether he wanted to stay on at Base Camp, but he replied that there seemed no point.

'If I can't take part in the climb, I think I'd rather get home to Jan and Daniel. There's just no point in hanging around here. It's not as if I could do anything to help you all.'

And so it was decided that Dick should set out for Lhasa in a few days' time, just before we returned to the climb. This would enable Charlie to keep him under observation a little longer and Dick to rest before his journey. We talked around the problem a while and then trailed back to our tents to read, write diaries or worry.

Pete observed:

Lying in my tent you can tell exactly who it is; Chris, from the snuffle breathing; Joe, from his groans. He's on his way over the gravel towards our windy bog. But Joe returns and arouses Charlie and they go and inspect his stool. I think; 'Oh no; blood in his stool; ulcer. Chris is out too, and Dick. I'll have to solo the North Col route, damn it!' Feel worried the whole trip is falling apart.

Charlie wrote in his diary:

And Joe, poor Joe. What on earth is going on? Dull, central abdominal pain,

*tarry black stool which can only mean blood. The easiest conclusion is an ulcer,
but he has a very bloody throat with a hard black crust right across the pharynx. I
suppose this could have seeped down and caused the problem. We'll have to wait
to see the outcome but clearly he cannot go anywhere with a bleeding bowel. I've
told him he mustn't go up unless he's really better.*

*And so we bathe our wounds and hope for a reasonable enough recovery to get
three up high and I suppose two on the summit. One would do. Trying to look at it
all objectively, I do not think we have a hope in hell. The days required to kill the
Pinnacles, added to the summit ridge, cannot be less than six and this is simply too
long without oxygen. I think:*

Pete could do it.

Joe probably could, but is ropey.

Chris has said he doesn't think he can and I'm sure he's right.

Dick can't because of illness.

Adrian has had severe chest pains.

*Me? Well, as usual, I'm apprehensive about being drawn into something much
too big for me and really a bit apprehensive about the North Col, particularly
as the weather is getting warmer. Still, I'll be pleased to have to go up there and
back.*

*This leaves two alternatives, either go for it, as Pete would like – or abandon it
and go for the Col route as a threesome. The first seems the purer – for two to climb
as far as they can on the Ridge – and I expect that is what will happen on the day.*

I was more optimistic than Charlie, feeling that Joe and Pete had a very
good chance of completing the Pinnacles. They had only to make a height
gain of about 300 metres over a distance of around a quarter of a mile. With
the knowledge that they could drop down to the North Col on the other side
and would not have to return over the Pinnacles, they could surely make the
traverse in a couple of days. We could even see what looked like an easy line
of traversing ledges that by-passed the Final Pinnacle.

I was less sanguine about their chances of reaching the summit, since it
did seem that they would need at least one night, maybe two, on the
Pinnacles before they reached the final section of the Ridge. It was
reasonably easy but there was a lot of it – a mile in horizontal distance and
450 metres of vertical height to gain. But even if they only managed to climb
the Pinnacles, this would have been a comparative success, for they would
have crossed the unclimbed part of the Ridge.

And what of my feelings? I was not depressed by my own failure and was
even relieved that I had made the decision to withdraw from the summit
bid. I had been so extended, so out of control. Now that I had finally
decided to drop back into a support role I felt a vast release of tension and
actually looked forward with an excited anticipation to our trip to the North
Col. This was something which seemed a useful contribution to the
expedition, was within my capabilities, and a goal in itself. In a letter to
Wendy I wrote: 'I have no regrets. I desperately want them to succeed and,

much more important, come back safely. I realise it's above my ceiling without oxygen and I want to get on with OUR LIVES!!! I only hope I haven't addled my brain already; I don't think so.'

We were all worried about possible brain damage through extended periods of effort at high altitude. We tried to make a joke of it, laughing about the grey cells we might have lost. Charlie had actually noticed some symptoms:

'Chris's short-term memory is appalling. He is capable of forgetting whole conversations we've had only a few hours previously. It's taken as a giggle, but I cannot really put this down to tiredness.'

The atmosphere that day had been oppressive. We were overwhelmed by the sudden change from slow, steady progress up the Ridge to the collapse of fifty per cent of the climbing team. But the following day, our second back at Base Camp, we had begun to pick ourselves up. Joe was feeling remarkably better, reassured that his black stools were probably caused by all the blood he had swallowed from his throat.

He quietly reassured Pete: 'Don't worry, I'll be OK. I'll be with you.'

I was beginning to make my own plans for our trip to the North Col. Dick borrowed a tele-photo lens so that he could go for one last walk and get some fresh pictures of Everest from around the ruined nunnery. It was a lovely clear morning, the sky, a far-flung vault of blue with Everest towering at the head of the valley with its characteristic cloud-banner blowing out from its summit. Dick felt as well and fit as he had ever done on the expedition and strode down the jeep track, resolving almost to walk out to Xegur, and pick up the jeep there. In that way he could remain close to the mountains for that brief period longer. The track wound round and down the glacial debris to the flat of the valley some three miles away and 150 metres below Base Camp. The ruined nunnery was just a short way up a slope and for the first time that morning he had to climb uphill.

His strength suddenly drained from him and he slowed down to little more than a crawl. He sat down on a rock; his vision became distorted, his heart pounded; he could hardly breathe. On the previous occasion he had not been frightened because he had not really known what was happening. Now he did. These were the symptoms of another stroke. He was alone; it would be hours before anyone found him. By that time it could be too late. 'Sit still, relax. You'll be all right.' He remembered that he had told Joe that he was going down to the nunnery. Someone would come and look for him.

He sat there for about quarter of an hour. His heart had returned to a more steady beat and he could now see clearly. He could get back to Base if he took it steadily. But he was so very, very weak. He dropped back to the track but it was now all uphill and seemed to go on for ever. He needed all his determination to just put one foot in front of the other.

Back in the base tent we were getting worried. It was past lunch time and Dick had been gone for several hours. We were just beginning to discuss sending out a search party, when he quietly slipped into the tent.

'Could I have a word with you?' he asked Charlie.

Once again everything was changed, turned up on end. There was now no question of Dick lingering at Base Camp for a few days, or of his being able to travel back on his own. Charlie was very worried about him having another more serious stroke and told us that he would have to accompany Dick at least as far as Chengdu. I could only agree, even though I was worried at losing our medical cover over the period of the summit bid. Joe and Pete would be pushing themselves so hard. After all only a few people had reached the summit of Everest without oxygen and they would be attempting something even more exacting. They would be several days above 8000 metres, pushing themselves to extremes.

'You will come straight back, of course,' I exhorted Charlie.

We broke up and wandered to our tents. Pete nudged Charlie. 'Thought you were going home, didn't you, you bugger!'

Mr Chen was, as always, calm and helpful, making sensible suggestions to help Dick and Charlie on their way. On the morning of 10th May, Dick, Charlie and Mr Yu piled into the jeep on the first stage of their journey. We all shook hands with Dick, slightly embarrassed, emotion pent up and inhibited, and then silently watched as the jeep bumped over the shingle road in the washed out grey of the early dawn.

Charlie recorded their journey:

On the evening of 11th May, Dick and I drove into Lhasa in a sandstorm. Dick had improved steadily and his health gave me no more cause for concern. He continued to make a complete recovery. We stopped for the night at the Lhasa rest house: the storm had settled and the air was warm. We had entered a different world; the cherries were in blossom and the willows in leaf; yaks ploughed, their decorative plumes waving in the wind. Tired and a little dejected, we flew to Chengdu next morning and were soon on the telephone, to London, to Hong Kong, to Peking and Cardiff. The Chinese could not have been more helpful – Everest Base Camp to Hong Kong in four days must be nearly a record. On the 13th, Dick and I parted rather solemnly at Chengdu Airport and I turned once again towards Everest. I suddenly wanted to go home.

Back in the big base tent the tiny size of our team really hit us. We missed Dick's strength and Charlie's caring cheerfulness. On a more material level, it was Charlie who baked the bread, who cooked the delicious fresh vegetable broths which we had so enjoyed at Advance Base. We were a sombre bunch but, at the same time, felt we could now start planning positively for the future. Joe and Pete were poring over photographs of the upper part of the Ridge, calculating heights and distances. There was a hidden level of communication between them from which, inevitably, I now felt excluded. And yet they never made me feel unwelcome. There was no resentment in their manner, nor was it recorded in their diaries. Joe in a letter to Maria, merely stated:

Chris is feeling a bit slow on the mountain . . . There is a big job for Pete and me to do but hopefully it could go well next time we go back up and if fortune, weather and spirit favour us we could be up the mountain in a few days from when we start . . . I'll write again soon, hopefully with more cheerful news, but as you can imagine – having come down for a rest – it has been quite a re-adjustment twice over in the last thirty-six hours to the new state of affairs and the situation does rather seem to dominate all.

And Pete to Hilary:

Chris more relaxed now he's changed his role, which is a great help to Joe and me. From the seven thirty meal onwards we keep each other amused with chat and alcohol for three hours. One more day of forgetfulness, and the problem returns and all is on our shoulders . . . Wish more letters from you would arrive; I need a bit more assurance before I launch on to this great, committing adventure.

We celebrated Joe's thirty-fourth birthday on the evening of 12th May, our last night at Base Camp. Our cook had risen to the occasion, baking a birthday cake and preparing a lavish feast. We decided to open one of our bottles of champagne but in the rarefied atmosphere the pressure difference was so great that most of the contents jetted out in a great streamer of foam, leaving little more than a few teaspoonfuls of wine. We opened another bottle, this time holding a plastic bucket ready to catch the exploding bubbles. It was a happy, boozy night with Joe in fine form, wryly funny, Pete gentle and very boyish, Adrian quiet and serious but with a twinkle of humour. 'Adrian's climbing career is rising like a phoenix,' said Pete. 'At this rate he'll be the first Englishman since the war to reach the North Col.' I had a feeling of immense affection for all three of my companions.

That night, in his tent, Pete wrote: 'A great birthday for Joe . . . whatever may happen on this trip, we'll be able to say we've had some good times.'

11: *They walked out of our lives*

13th–21st May/Chris Bonington

Back at Advance Base the big green tent was as bleak and gloomy as ever, with the wind screaming down the Rongbuk Glacier, clutching and buffeting the fabric of the walls. We had walked up that day, Pete, Joe and Adrian covering the distance in a good fast time, with me bringing up the rear, trailing in a couple of hours later.

Our original plan had been for Pete and Joe to set out the following morning, but now they were having second thoughts. They talked around it and eventually decided to have a rest day. It proved a wise choice, for the 14th was cold and blustery. There was not much organising to do, for much of the food and all the climbing gear was already in place in the Third Snow Cave or at the high point. We spent a quiet day, most of it in our own tents, reading, writing our diaries or just sleeping.

Pete wrote:

Not missed anything today – a blustery night and though it became still first thing this morning, it started snowing soon after and has been blowing about wildly all morning . . . I slept deeply and got up about ten thirty. Had a big breakfast, cereal and fried ham. But you do feel different up here, a slight heaviness in the head. You do deteriorate.

Perhaps this general bad weather will subside, and a great spell of sunshine lasting five days will arrive. Chris is much more relaxed on this trip since he changed his role – cheerful and jokey and supportive.

The 15th dawned clear though windy. Pete and Joe fussed around with final preparations, packing their rucksacks and putting in a few last-minute goodies. Then suddenly they were ready, crampons on, rope tied, set to go. I think we were all trying to underplay the moment.

'See you in a few days.'

'We'll call you tonight at six o'clock.'

'Good luck.'

And then they were off, plodding up the little ice slope immediately beyond the camp, through flurries of wind-driven snow. They were planning to move straight through to the Second Snow Cave, to avoid spending longer than absolutely necessary at altitude. This would mean they would reach the Third Cave on their second day, and then on the third they hoped to traverse the Pinnacles and reach the North Ridge. If they could do this they would be in a very good position to make their bid for the summit on the fourth or fifth day. To have any chance of success they had to keep to this schedule, for they could not afford to spend more than two nights above 8250 metres before going for the summit.

Adrian and I were hoping to find a way up to the North Col that same day. We left shortly after the others and our route took us up the piled rocks of the moraine past the site of the French Camp, the skeleton of an old frame tent a reminder of the former expedition. They had been defeated by the North Ridge and it was as if the mess they had left was a futile revenge on the mountain, or was it that they had no feeling for the empty beauty of the glacier and peaks around them, for their rubbish was spread all the way up the East Rongbuk Glacier?

We followed the thinning moraine to a rocky corner which forced us on to the glacier itself. It was time to rope up. The glacier was easy, sloping gradually in a series of gentle waves to the great wall of the North Col. To our surprise, the way was marked with bamboo poles, to which still clung the shreds of yellow flags. Had these, too, been left by the French, or perhaps by the Japanese the previous year? It meant that we could plod, unthinking, towards our goal. But as we approached it, the wall at the end of the valley loomed ever steeper. I had thought of 'just nipping up to the North Col,' but now I began to realise that I had underestimated it. Adrian's climbing experience was strictly limited. He had come with us to the South West Face of Everest in 1975 to help run our Advance Base since, as an officer in the Gurkhas, he spoke fluent Nepali, but he had done practically no ice climbing. At the end of the expedition he had spent a night at our fourth camp at 7300 metres, then, in a hasty evacuation in the dark, had very nearly lost his life, when he descended much more slowly than the Sherpas who had accompanied him and had lost the route. When we had reached him at around midnight, he was beginning to show signs of hypothermia and certainly would not have lasted much longer. He had done very little snow and ice climbing since then and had only envisaged being in a support role on our expedition this time. Nevertheless, he was glad of his new task, commenting:

At last I'm doing something positive and feel better and stronger than I have done for over three weeks; even the pain in my chest seems to have subsided to a dull ache. And yet despite my renewed vigour and enthusiasm I'm not without fear, for the North Col has claimed a fair number of casualties in the last sixty years. The first time I set eyes on it, I thought, 'I'm bloody glad I'm not going up there.' But here I am.

Adrian quickly showed that he was fresher than I. He had a spring in his step that I lacked. After an hour's walk we reached the crest of a slight wave in the glacier and stopped to examine the route. I could see that the line of flags led up to a smooth convex slope of ice that continued up towards a wide snow ramp which, in turn, led up to a barrier of sérac walls. There seemed a way through these, but it was undoubtedly complex. To the left of the Col, the slope was uninterrupted by séracs or crevasses, but it was very much steeper. This was the route that Mr Chen had recommended and the one that Reinhold Messner had used when he climbed the mountain solo, but it looked rather steep for someone as inexperienced as Adrian. The easiest angled route was on the right but this was obviously threatened by avalanche.

I was finally influenced by the presence of the marker flags and followed these to the foot of the ice slope. Once there we quickly realised that this was a route only for a party with plenty of rope to fix in position. The ice, though not steep, was smooth and polished. We retreated and took stock once again. I decided to go for the left-hand route, took a wide circuit round the foot of the face, and started up the slope. By this time the day had galloped away and it was now nearly four in the afternoon. We had arranged to call Pete and Joe on the radio at six thirty, but had left it back at Advance Base – a good excuse for retreat.

That day Pete and Joe had made a good fast time to the Second Cave and told us they felt they were going well. I told them that we would try to reach the North Col the next day and arranged to open up once again at six thirty in the evening. The following morning we took with the radio, a tent and some food, hoping to dump the gear on the Col, so that when we moved up the following day we should only have to carry our sleeping bags and personal gear.

We quickly reached the previous day's high point, but almost immediately found ourselves on steep ground, crossing ice covered by powdery, insubstantial snow. This led up to a bergschrund, with a long stride on to a steep wall of crusty snow; certainly not the easy slog that I had promised Adrian. How about getting back down? Above, the slope smoothed out, but it was consistently steep. In addition, some 450 metres above us, a series of huge cornices loomed threateningly. If they collapsed we were in their direct line of fall.

I glanced across to the right and saw a route we could have taken to turn the convex ice slope that had deterred us the previous day. The angle was altogether easier over there and much more within the range of Adrian's experience. But to reach it we should have to go beneath a shattered sérac wall, over a slope littered with huge ice blocks. It seemed worth it and I headed across, with Adrian in tow. He was none too happy:

My confidence in Chris's ability to select the safest route received a set-back today. We had begun our ascent slightly to the left when Chris decided to cut back under a horrendous-looking sérac. 'Quite stable,' says he, while I peered into the bowels of this monster, muttering the Buddhist mantra 'Om mani padme hum' faster than a Tibetan can twirl his prayer wheel!

But this took us on to an easier line that led up through the centre of the slope. The snow now became quite soft and deep, for we were on the lee side, but the angle was sufficiently easy for Adrian to take over the lead. He was undoubtedly going more strongly than I and I was very glad to let him do the trail-breaking for a while until once again the slope steepened. I went out in front, cramponing up steep hard snow.

We had now reached the area of sérac walls in the upper part of the face. I had observed what seemed to be a gangway between two of the séracs which eventually led to the final slopes just below the North Col. I struck up this, stepping very gingerly over some windslab to the top of the slope, and was appalled to find a huge, moat-like crevasse between me and the sérac wall, stretching as far as I could see in either direction. I first had a look to the left, but the crest narrowed to a fin-like arête, falling away into another giddy drop. Glancing back to the right, I noticed a ladder hanging precariously from the sheer ice wall on the other side of the crevasse. If we could only reach it. This surely must have been the route used by the French. I followed the lip of the crevasse until I was opposite the ladder. The crevasse was about two and a half metres wide at this point and another ladder, like a drawbridge, was dangling provocatively from the other side, just out of reach. But it was getting late. The sun had already dropped behind the North Col, leaving us in cold shadow. The depths of the crevasse were blue-black, its lip crumbling. I moved tentatively on to a fragile snow bridge that spanned the chasm.

'Watch the rope, Adrian, the whole bloody lot could go.'

But what if I did get to the other side? I should have about four or five metres of sheer ice to traverse to reach the foot of the ladder, and how secure was that? I was tired and frightened.

'It's nearly six thirty, Chris. Hadn't you better call the lads?'

Respite! I fled from the brink of the crevasse, and traversed back along its edge so that we could see round the corner and have a direct line of sight with the crest of the North East Ridge.

'Hello Snow Cave Three, this is Chris just below the North Col, can you hear me? Over.'

There was no reply. We tried again a few minutes later and Pete's voice came through, telling us that they had reached the Third Snow Cave in good time and would be going for the Pinnacles the next morning. I replied that we had not managed to reach the North Col that day, that we would be having a rest day tomorrow, and would move up to the North Col on the 18th, ready to receive them if they came down that way. We arranged to have a radio call at three o'clock the following afternoon and then again at six p.m. A hurried 'good luck' for the morrow and the radio was dead.

We dumped all the gear we had carried up on the lip of the crevasse, marked it with an alloy wand and started down. We were both very tired and Adrian, who had never been on snow as steep as this without the reassurance of a fixed rope, was understandably nervous. On the way we were able to avoid the dangerous sérac wall by making a long traverse towards Changtse. Even here we had some moments of excitement, when the snow ran out and Adrian had to pick his way down the smooth icy crest. He slipped, but fortunately I was ready, and was able to hold him. Eventually we reached the comparative safety of the glacier and were able to plod through the gathering gloom back to the rocky moraine. We trailed slowly back to the camp, reaching it in the dark. It had been a fourteen-hour day and we were both exhausted. That night we were too tired to cook any food. We just melted some snow for tea, and collapsed into our sleeping bags.

It was always difficult getting up before the sun warmed the tent, which happened at about nine. Even then, I lay for a long time in a stupor before thirst and hunger drove me out of the warmth of my sleeping bag. It was another perfect day, cloudless, almost windless, a pleasure to be out. I staggered over to the mess tent and for the first time that morning, peered through the telescope. I started at the snow shoulder, behind which hid the Third Snow Cave. No sign of them there, so I swung the telescope along the crest of the Ridge leading to the First Pinnacle. Still no sign. Could they have overslept? And then I saw them, two small, distinct figures, at the high point they had previously reached on the First Pinnacle. To get there they must either have travelled very fast, or perhaps had even set out before dawn. They certainly knew that they had to cover a lot of ground that day, for to have a good chance of reaching the summit they had to reach Point 8393 that evening.

The image through the telescope was so sharp I could actually see their limbs. For the rest of the day, either Adrian or I watched through the telescope as Pete and Joe slowly made their way along the Ridge. But now their progress had slowed down. They were on new, and presumably, difficult ground. We assumed they were leaving a fixed rope behind them for they had with them about three hundred metres of rope. Their slowness was not surprising. They were now at around 8250 metres above sea level. They must have had around fifteen kilos each on their backs, with their sleeping bags, tent, stove, food, fuel and climbing gear. It was difficult to tell how hard the climbing was but I suspect it was harder than they had anticipated. I wondered if anyone had ever climbed to that standard at that height before. They were now higher than all but five peaks in the world.

We spent the day cooking, drinking and eating, but constantly going back to the telescope to gaze up at those tiny figures. I longed for three o'clock, so that we could turn on the sound, have some kind of contact with them, hear how they were, what the climbing was like – but most of all just to hear them. It was five to three. I opened up the radio and started calling.

'Hello climbing team, hello climbing team, this is Advance Base, do you read me? Over?'

The set crackled in my hand, but it was just some distant voices speaking Chinese. The Pinnacles, etched black against the sky, were stark and jagged. I tried again. It was now past three but there was still no reply. I was not unduly worried. Perhaps their set had failed, but more likely they were so engrossed in the climbing they either forgot to open up or just did not have time. I could clearly see one figure on the Ridge, outlined against the sky, half way between the crest of the First Pinnacle, and the black tooth of the Second. The other figure was just below the skyline, moving very slowly.

We now called on the half hour through the rest of the afternoon but there was no reply. At nine that evening, the sun already hidden behind Everest, we looked up at them for the last time and called them yet again on the radio. One figure was silhouetted in the fading light on the small col immediately below the Second Pinnacle, whilst the other figure was still moving to join him.

They had been on the go for fourteen hours. It was only twenty minutes or so before dark, so they had to find somewhere to spend the night at the foot of the Second Pinnacle, either a snow cave, or more likely a small ledge cut out of the snow on which they could pitch the tent. But what was it like up there? The Ridge was obviously narrow and the slopes on either side seemed steep, but there was plenty of snow on the eastern side. The only problem, perhaps, could be that it was too soft and insubstantial.

We had our evening meal, looked up at the Ridge, whose black serrated edge could be seen clearly against the inky blue of the clear, star-studded sky. There was no twinkling of a light and presumably they were camped or holed up on the other side. I slept deeply that night but next morning immediately went over to the telescope.

There was no sign of them. Perhaps they were already on their way. It was another brilliant, clear day and the absence of a snow plume from the summit indicated that there was little wind to trouble them. We knew that they would be out of sight on the other side of the Ridge for a hundred metres or so, since on the north side the way was barred by the sheer rocky buttresses of the Second Pinnacle. I had a feeling that they would try to get back on to the north as quickly as possible, both because the snow on the east would probably be insecure and also to have some kind of contact with us, even if their radio was no longer working. There also seemed to be interconnecting ledges across rocky slopes on this side.

At this stage we were not unduly worried. We leisurely packed our rucksacks, had one last brew, and then, leaving a note for Charlie to let him know what was happening, set off for the North Col. This time we retraced our descent route and made steady, uneventful progress. I had brought with me a pair of binoculars and every ten minutes or so I gazed up at the Ridge, hoping to see Joe and Pete. From the slopes leading up to the Col we had an excellent view. Beyond the Second Pinnacle there was a very small col. The crest of the Ridge then levelled out for what, I estimated, were about three rope lengths, before dropping away to the col beneath the Final Pinnacle. We knew from photographs that they then had to come on to this side of the Ridge, for there was a sheer rock buttress on the eastern side. To the north there was a line of ledges which we thought would give easy access on to the North Face.

I explored each point where I thought they might come into sight and then swung the lenses back down the Ridge. Our field of view was so good that they would have been clearly visible had they returned to the crest or northern side of the Ridge. But there was nothing. Just rock and snow and ice. I could not stop myself praying that they were all right. I found myself crying in the intensity of an anxiety that had crept up on me almost unawares. I chided myself. Nothing to worry about yet. They're just on the other side of the Ridge.

We were now on the ramp leading up the centre of the North Col. Our steps from two days ago were covered with wind-blown snow and again I was very happy to let Adrian do the trail-breaking. It was six in the evening before we reached our previous high point. I took a tentative look at a narrow arête of snow. It looked feasible, but steep and frightening, something to be attempted in the morning when we'd be feeling fresh.

'Come on, Adrian, we'll stop here for the night. It's safe enough with this crevasse between us and the slope.'

I started digging a platform beside the crevasse. Adrian was appalled at the exposure of our perch but I tried to reassure him that it was perfectly safe. 'Once in the tent you can forget the drop.'

It was a wonderful dusk, the sky cloudless, with hardly a breath of wind. To one side the North East Ridge was black and massive, while below us the East Rongbuk Glacier swept away in a vast white highway. On the other side of the glacier stretched the gentle snow peaks flanking the Lhakpa La and behind them towered the solid rocky triangle of Khartaphu. The very peace of the scene was soothing. I was glad to be high once again, glad to be climbing with Adrian and sharing with him our own modest adventure of reaching the North Col.

The following morning we struck the tent and I set out along the fragile crest of the arête which we hoped would by-pass the crevasse. As so often happens, it was easier than it looked, and although it steepened into a nearly vertical drop into the huge crevasse below us, I had the security of the rope paid out by Adrian. Cutting big bucket steps, I worked my way down, then shouted to Adrian to anchor the rope so that he could follow. We now had the rope in position for our return. Soon we had both cautiously abseiled down it and were able to break out on to the easy ramp we had seen from below. Once more I was pleased for Adrian to take the lead on straightforward ground. As we went up, we were still searching the Ridge every few minutes but still there was no sign. Although we were getting anxious, we could not help enjoying the sensation of being on new ground, of finding our way up to the North Col. There were intriguing reminders of our predecessors. An old cable-laid nylon rope hung from a huge overhanging boss of snow. Could it have been left by the Chinese in 1975? Further up, by a formidable, narrow ice chimney, projected a butane gas cylinder, French 1981 vintage, no doubt. This route seemed too hard for us and we continued up the ramp to the foot of an acutely-angled snow slope that seemed to lead to the crest of the Ridge. Once again I went into the lead, kicking my way up the steep, but secure snow, until suddenly my head poked over the crest. I had reached the North Col.

It was a sharp knife-edge, dropping away steeply on the other side with the fresh vista of Pumo Ri, shapely and elegant, in the near distance and behind it the great bulk of Cho Oyu. I moved cautiously along the knife-edge to where it broadened into an easy slope, and buried a deadman snow anchor. While Adrian jumared up the rope I was able to look around. The ridge opened out into a wide dome just above the lowest point of the Col. It would provide both a good camp site and an excellent viewpoint of the North East Ridge. In the concentration and very real joy of climbing that final pitch to the Col, there had been no room for my growing worry about Pete and Joe, but now it came creeping back. I got out the binoculars and searched the line of Ridge again but to no avail.

But what of the Americans in the Great Gully of the North Face? I started searching for them and picked out a collection of tents, tiny coloured boxes, clinging beneath a sheer sérac wall. There was no sign of movement, but a line of tracks wound sinuously across the slope, taking a route round the huge icefall that barred the Great Gully at about half height. There was another camp, tucked below a rocky overhang just near the side of the couloir, and I could just discern some more tracks. Surely they also would be going for the summit in such perfect weather?

By this time Adrian had joined me. He shared with me a sense of elation very similar to that which I experience on reaching a summit. I suppose it was because this was our chosen objective. Just after he arrived we saw two tiny figures descending the fixed ropes on the American route. Could they be Pete and Joe, who had somehow got across on to the North Face without us seeing them? But this was clutching at straws. Our logic quickly told us that these were Americans, perhaps on their way down from a successful summit bid.

We dug out a platform for the tent and spent the rest of the day taking it in turns to examine the North East Ridge. It was now 19th May and I was very worried. Pete and Joe had been out of sight for two nights and almost two days. From this viewpoint we could see just how short a distance they would have had to cover before we could expect them to come into sight on our side of the Ridge after turning the Second Pinnacle.

That afternoon, Adrian picked out some movement at Advance Base. Could it be *them*? Could they somehow have retreated all the way down without us seeing them? But no. There were three figures. It could be the American skiers, or perhaps it was Charlie who had come up with some Tibetans. We opened up on the radio at six o'clock. There was no reply from Pete or Joe, but Charlie, reassuring and cheerful, came on the air. I immediately told him of my fears. Charlie recalls:

At six p.m. on 19th I had a crackly radio link with the Col. I was about to berate Chris about the mess but his message was anxious, high pitched, almost unintelligible. They had not seen them . . . 'I am concerned . . .'

'*I share your concern,' I replied.*

I share your concern . . . my world of elation was quick-frozen, replaced, not yet by sorrow or pain, but by a curious reality. I was in a high camp, with two Tibetans for the night. Three miles away on the North East Ridge something had happened or was happening. Two miles away on the North Col Chris and Adrian were safe. We were 6000 miles from home. I talked bleakly to my diary:

> *The Ridge is very much a spectator sport from down here up to the Second Pinnacle. Then there is obviously some dead ground. I'm not sure how the view compares from the North Col. I think we must prepare for a disaster. But there is still hope. If the situation is the same tomorrow I shall have almost given up.*
>
> *However, we had all this on Kongur last year and everyone was OK.[1] On the positive side they could have shot off early on the 18th, gone out of sight, conquered the 'great problem'. On the 19th they could be out of sight still, in all probability camped between the two steps, summit tomorrow and back to the North Col.*
>
> *The outcome will be quite simple. They'll either come bouncing in or drag themselves in in various degrees of injury or illness: or, we'll never see them again. I cannot really accept them as lost, but then it took a while for Mick's loss to sink in.[2] Oh God.*

I did not sleep well that night and as soon as it was light enough I was gazing up anxiously through the binoculars. Another perfect day but still no sign. We opened up on the radio on the hour throughout the day, but with little hope of a reply since it was unlikely that we should hear them unless they were in direct line of sight. I now searched not only the crest but the glacier at its foot, just in case they had fallen.

That night Adrian went outside for one last look up at the Ridge.

'Chris, come and have a look at this, I think I can see something. It could be a tent.'

He handed me the binoculars.

'It's about a third of the way along the Ridge, above and beyond the Pinnacles, just below the crest. Look, there are three slight bumps. Go down from the left-hand one. There's a bit of a gully, and there it is, on a kind of ledge. It's just a little orange blob. It could be a tent, couldn't it?'

It was certainly on the line from the Final Pinnacle on to the North Face. Then why hadn't we seen them? They would have been in view, moving slowly, for a long time. But that little orange blob was a slender strand of hope. I pushed logical doubts aside. That could be Pete and Joe. Perhaps they had reached the top and were on their way down. They could be with us tomorrow. Neither Adrian nor I slept that night. I imagined what they would have to say, what they had done, how they would look, convincing

[1] The summit party were out of contact for ten days in 1981.
[2] Mick Burke's death on Everest in 1975.

myself that it was undoubtedly their tent and that they were on their way down. The night crept away so very slowly. We had arranged a call to Charlie at eight and I expressed my hope.

'There's a faint ray of hope. Last night Adrian saw a small red patch that could be a Sumitomo tent. It's on about the right line. But we haven't seen any figures and, of course, it's possible that it's a ruined tent from a previous expedition. It's on rock rather than snow, which means it doesn't stand out quite so well. It's not a hundred per cent but at least it's hopeful. Over.'

But as the light on the North Face improved and we gazed at the distant little blob, our hopes dwindled. There was no sign of movement. It was the wrong colour, being orange when the outer of the Sumitomo was a deep red and its inner a bright yellow. It was also the wrong shape, looking more square than domed. It was perhaps a box tent abandoned by the French the previous year. The weather had been so clear and our viewpoint so good, that surely we should have seen them if they had reached the end of the Pinnacles? Our hopes vanished and despair set in. They had now been out of sight for four days – four days to cover a distance of about three rope lengths at the least, eight or so at the very most. Four nights above 8250 metres. If their progress had been so slow, surely they would have decided to retreat. We had already seen the effects of spending four nights at 7850 metres.

The only explanation must be that a catastrophe had occurred. What if one of them had fallen and was injured? Surely the other would have retraced his steps to signal us for help, particularly since we assumed they had left a line of fixed rope behind them? It would have meant retreating only two or three rope lengths. Or could both of them have fallen sick or be so incapacitated by exhaustion that neither could move? This seemed unlikely. They were well acclimatised, and though perhaps tired from our long siege, they knew how to pace themselves and had been at these altitudes without oxygen before, on Kangchenjunga and K_2. One of them could perhaps have collapsed, but not two. That left a grim interpretation. That they were both dead. Either one had fallen, pulling off the other, or perhaps one of those fragile ice flutings had collapsed, sweeping both of them down the huge Kangshung Face. I could remember its immense scale, just how steep the upper part of the Ridge had seemed, and how insubstantial and dangerous Dick had found that pitch on the First Pinnacle.

Below us Charlie had also spent a sleepless night.

I was washed over by different waves of emotion. I fought with pain because I loved them. They were the personification of what I had once wanted to be, but I had not that combination of physique, skill and drive to push high on great peaks. They courted danger, yes, in the huge scale of the undertaking but not because they were reckless. Not Pete and Joe. There are, I think, some climbers who can – in the fervour of their ambition, intoxicated by danger and excited by the prospect of success – push aside all fear and feelings, take great risks and, moving fast, often alone, survive enough times to gain a reputation. To me these climbers are as one of the faces of Buddha, who lived as a hermit practising extreme asceticism, emaciated beyond measure before gaining enlightenment by this supreme sacrifice. I wondered if Pete and Joe, like Buddha returning after his enlightenment, would come back to the world of man and accept the dish of fresh curds from the village girl on the Full Moon Day of May. For Peter and Joe there was, I feel, that Middle Way: they believed that hard high-altitude climbing was a reasonable sport within mountaineering. Statistically dangerous, yes, but with care, stealth and speed, within reason. They had affirmed their faith in high altitude by repeated visits, they knew and respected the arena of avalanche, storm and stonefall. They had pushed hard and fast at the summit of Kangchenjunga, retreated in the face of avalanches from K2. They were wily and sometimes very frightened. They never showed self-indulgent elation when successful.

I talked it over with Adrian and then at mid-day with Charlie. There seemed nothing to gain by staying on the North Col. We left the tent in place, anchored to a snow shovel and its valance securely wedged down with snow. We also left the radio, the cooking gear, all the remaining food and a note welcoming them back and telling them what we had done.

We held ourselves tightly in control. Although I had very little hope of their survival I could not bring myself to admit it. Besides, we were still on the mountain and needed all our concentration to return safely to Advance Base. By the time we reached the sérac wall where I had left a fixed rope, the clouds had engulfed us and the wind was beginning to whip stinging snowflakes into our faces. Adrian, who wears glasses, was almost blinded as they misted up. He was also feeling the debilitating effects of spending three nights at around 7000 metres. We were both very, very tired as we stumbled down the slope, thankful for the marker wands we had placed to guide us down.

Back on the glacier we could begin to relax, and then, having reached the rocky moraine, we were able to take off the rope and walk down in our own time. I pulled ahead, forcing myself over the broken rocks covered in fresh snow, to get back to the camp. At last it was in sight and Charlie was coming towards me.

'They've had it. I'm sure they've had it,' I muttered.

'I know.'

We held each other and wept.

12: A fruitless search

21st May–1st June/Chris Bonington

It was all so familiar. Adrian sat quietly in his usual corner. Charlie cut some bread. The big kettle bubbled on top of three Gaz stoves, the pressure cooker hissed quietly, the canvas of the big green tent rattled in the wind. Books, gloves, karabiners, cine equipment, packages of food were piled on the boxes round the cluttered stone table. Some of the gear belonged to Pete and Joe. We had to decide what to do and the very urgency of this demand was a therapy in itself, helping us to control our grief.

In front of us was the picture file, so meticulously collected by Pete before the expedition, some of them from the prewar expeditions, others taken by the Americans who had attempted the Kangshung Face the previous year. The stark black and white pictures emphasised the ferocious steepness of those snow flutings on the East Face. We thrashed over the possibilities and arguments that we had all been grappling with in the last few days.

'You know, when you look at that face,' I said, 'it's just great clusters of snow plastered on to very steep rock so that the whole lot could come away. If they did fall, it wouldn't have been a hundred metres, it'd be nearer a thousand. It's horrendously steep.'

'But it is just possible, isn't it, Chris, that they could have survived in some huge slide of snow, and could somehow have got all the way down on to the Kangshung Glacier?' said Charlie.

'It'd be a one in a million chance,' I replied. 'I just can't believe they could have survived a fall on that, and even if they did, just look how steep the bottom is. They'd never get down it.'

'But it's still just possible,' persisted Charlie. 'Look at Messner on Nanga Parbat. There've been other instances as well when people have fallen and got down into another valley. However unlikely it is I think we must go up the Kangshung Valley.'

'I agree,' I said, 'but we've also got to keep this side under observation, just in case they do get back this way. Someone's going to have to sit it out here as well.'

'I don't mind doing that,' volunteered Adrian.

'You know, I suppose we should really go back up the Ridge itself and try to reach their high point.'

'Come on, Chris, be realistic,' said Charlie. 'I don't think Adrian or I could make it, and for that matter, could you? And anyway, would we see anything?'

'I know. I know all that. But you can't help feeling that you should. And I suppose that's the question everyone will ask. We've got to tell Hilary and Maria what we've done. We've got to try to eliminate every possibility, however strongly we feel they're dead, however certain we are that they've fallen down the Kangshung Face.'

'Yeah, but even if you managed to get all the way to the Second Pinnacle, how much would you see? Would it confirm anything?' asked Adrian.

'I suppose if we found a broken rope at their high point, that'd be some kind of confirmation. But at least we'd know they weren't there, that they hadn't collapsed from exhaustion or were sick. But quite honestly, I don't see how they could be. I could believe that one of them might be sick, but not both of them. They'd have such a short distance to get back into sight, and they should have had a fixed rope as well. I'm afraid the only real explanation is that they've both fallen.

'The trouble is as well that, unless we actually reached their high point, we'd learn no more than we know now. And you're right; quite honestly I don't think I could make it again up to the Pinnacles. I was shattered just getting up to the North Col. There's no way you or Charlie could be expected to go on to the ridge without any fixed ropes.'

'Well then, it's the Kangshung Valley,' said Charlie.

'I agree. I think we'll see more from there with the telescope than we ever would on the Ridge itself.'

We discussed the plan in detail. To reach the Kangshung Valley we could have followed the American skiers over the Lhakpa La and Karpo La, but this would have meant carrying mountaineering gear and coming back the same way. If Pete and Joe had somehow managed to get down into the Kangshung Valley, it was most unlikely that they would be in a fit state to climb back over a high pass. On the other hand, if we returned to Base Camp we could drive to the Kharta Valley and trek over the Langma La, into the Kangshung Valley. At the same time we could warn Mr Chen of our fears.

This raised another problem. We needed to keep news of our fears to ourselves until we had exhausted every possibility. We talked late into the night, trying to think of every eventuality, before collapsing into drugged sleep.

Next morning Charlie and I set off, leaving Adrian to his solitary vigil. It was typical of his selflessness that he had volunteered to stay. He was going to remain there, keeping the Ridge under observation until 28th May, when we promised to send up the yaks to carry down our equipment. He was to have a week of complete isolation clearing up the camp, burying our rubbish and packing loads.

On the way back to Base Camp I wanted to make a diversion to the American Camp, to tell them of our fears and to ask them to keep an eye out for our two friends. There was just a chance that they might see something from high on the North Ridge during a summit bid.

Charlie and I walked together to the junction with the Central Rongbuk

Glacier. He pushed on towards Base Camp while I turned south up the side of the glacier. I felt very much alone. 'It's not far at all,' Charlie had said, but the glacier seemed to stretch away endlessly. There was just an occasional paint-daubed rock to indicate the route. And what if no-one was there? If they were all away climbing? At last I noticed a little cluster of tents on the glacier below. I had over-shot. There was no sign of any activity and the site had a desolate, empty feel to it. I approached, full of dread that there would be nobody around. A head appeared from a tent doorway, and soon I was sitting among friends in their mess tent. I had indeed been lucky for they had come down from their Advance Base that day, and were going back up the next.

I told them of our fears for Pete and Joe; they heard me out and then told me that they also had had a tragedy. Just a few days before on 15th May, Marty Hoey, the only girl in the team, had fallen to her death. Four of them had been climbing the fixed ropes to establish their top camp for a summit bid, when somehow, she had fallen out of her harness, all the way down the Central Gully. I could see they were still stunned by what happened, though they had decided to make one more bid for the summit. I expressed my sympathy and asked them to keep an eye out for Joe and Pete if they did manage to reach the crest of the Ridge. They promised to do so, and invited me to stay the night at their camp, for it was now past six in the evening.

But I did not want to stay. I felt the need to be in our own little world at Base Camp and, by walking there that night, driving myself to the point of exhaustion so that I might get some sleep.

It was dark by the time I got back and Charlie had already told Mr Chen. There was no criticism, no questioning, only sympathy and offers of help. Next morning we made our plans in detail. Mr Yu was going to accompany us when we took the truck round to the Kharta Valley. In the meantime Mr Chen was going to organise our flights back to Hong Kong, reassuring us that in no circumstances would our fears about Pete and Joe be revealed prematurely.

On 24th May we drove the hundred miles on bumpy dirt roads to the Kharta Valley. It was now summer, and the fields were lush with newly sprouting barley. We were following the broad valley that drains the Rongbuk Glacier, the Dzakar Chhu which curls round to the east into the great Arun River and flows through the Himalaya into Nepal. The village of Kharta is described as a leafy paradise in the early Everest books, such a contrast from Rongbuk that several expeditions seem to have been lured this way because of its beauty. Now the terrain has changed with the woods thin and many fields barren, the result of ruthless deforestation for fuel. We paused at the Kharta Commune Headquarters – a soulless, corrugated courtyard in a windswept dusty valley. Where were the hedges of rhododendrons, where were the flowers? Trees had been demolished here on a huge scale. We bought potatoes, arranged porters for the next day and drove on six miles up the Kharta Valley.

Suddenly, around a corner we saw some familiar tents. The American ski team were pitched on a grassy bank by the Kharta stream. Ned, Jan, Jim and Rick greeted us wildly at first – they had become great friends – then we told them tersely of our fears. They asked questions, voiced their sympathy.

Whilst we had been on the Ridge they had not been idle; they had crossed the Lhakpa La and Karma La, dropping into the Kangshung Valley, aiming to descend it and then turn north along the Arun Gorge at a village marked on the map at Sakyetang. A track was also shown, running down the Kharta Valley floor, through Sakyetang and on over lower hills to Kharta. They had searched for a week for this route, battled through forests of rhododendrons and finally, short of food, they had turned back in an attempt to find another route out. Luckily they had met several porters whom their Chinese staff had sent from Kharta. These guided them back over a 4870-metre pass, the Langma La. As far as we could establish there had never been a route down the Karma to Sakyetang and the entrance to this valley from the east can only be reached over the Langma La, crossed by Mallory and Bullock in 1921. This was the route we were to follow – entailing a three-day journey to the Kangshung Glacier.

Charlie and I pitched our tent and started cooking some supper. The four Americans were obviously in conference, and Ned eventually walked over and told us that they would be happy to keep us company in our search even though it would mean retracing their steps. We were delighted. Not only would it mean that we should have someone with us who knew the way but, perhaps even more important, they would be able to help in the remote event of a rescue.

We set out the following day, accompanied by three cheerful Tibetans who were going to act as guides and porters. The terrain was so different from the Rongbuk side. On the valley floor azaleas were in bud, rhododendrons already in flower, while alpine flowers were beginning to bloom in the grassy meadows beneath the Langma La.

On the second day we crossed the pass, getting a glimpse of the huge snow-clad Kangshung Face of Everest for a few minutes through the clouds. We descended to the glacier past frozen lakes and then over hillsides covered in coarse, tussocky grass and azaleas. To the south the walls of Chomo Lonzo and Pethangtse fell precipitately to the valley floor, huge spires looming out of the mists. Sometimes we caught glimpses of Everest some ten miles up the valley but with a high rainfall the Karma Valley is often filled with cloud, sucked in by the huge face which blocks its western end.

On the third night we arrived at the head of the valley, Base Camp site for the 1981 American Expedition that had attempted the Kangshung Face. It had clouded over that morning and the mist was clinging to the tops of the moraine ridges all around us, hiding the mountain peaks and revealing only a desolate expanse of jumbled rock, dirty grey ice and dark crevasses. We looked with distaste at the western litter of empty boxes, torn paperbacks and tins scattered over a meadow of sparse grass on the side of the glacier. The boxes provided fuel for a huge bonfire. The Great Carton Festival, Ned called it. He had an infectious enthusiasm that had lifted Charlie and me from our preoccupied introspection but that night, gazing into the patterns of the flames, I felt the tension mounting within me.

Would the fog clear during the night? Would we see anything? I didn't know whether to dread seeing no trace at all, or to be confronted with irrefutable evidence of what had happened. And what of Adrian? He was on his own in that tomb-like tent, so full of memories. He couldn't escape into the brief, if brittle, laughter that we were able to share with our companions. The fire was dying, the rubbish that had fuelled it exhausted. We trailed back to the tents, and I quickly dropped off to sleep, to be woken by Ned in the pallid pre-dawn. It was 28th May. The fog had cleared and the huge Kangshung Face was now clearly visible at the head of the valley.

We mounted the telescope on a tripod and took turns to stare through it. I could pick out the shoulder where we had dug the Third Snow Cave, the First Pinnacle and the col below the Second Pinnacle where, eleven days before, I had seen that small figure outlined against the darkening sky. Near-vertical ice flutings dropped away below the Pinnacles, sheer runnels swept clear of snow. Below were the tiers of séracs, icefalls and finally rock buttresses which form the 3000-metre-high face. Nothing moved other than the occasional avalanche. There was no sign of Pete and Joe. We walked back quietly, often apart, wrapped in thought. There was little to say. The faint hope we had lived with for over two weeks was now gone.

Three days later Charlie and I were back at Base Camp. Adrian had arrived from Advance Base: he had no news. There remained a final act. Charlie had chosen a large slate from near the 1924 memorial and during the evenings had picked and chiselled away at a simple epitaph. As in 1924 the Tibetans built a cairn upon a hill near Base Camp. We placed the tablet and stood silently, tearful in the wind. Next day we left to bring our bad news home.

Epilogue

To Wendy Bonington in Cumbria and Martin Henderson in Jardines' London office fell the task of breaking the news. There was already a sense of foreboding in the air. We had sent no news for three weeks at a critical stage of the expedition, perhaps explicable enough in itself. Whilst our unhappy tale remained a private one, the details of our probable travel arrangements did not. Hilary, Ruth, Maria, Wendy and Frenda were anxious when they heard that Chris was 'due to fly to Peking on 5th June'. There was no news of success or failure. Experienced expedition watchers, they felt strongly that something was gravely amiss.

Dick travelled to Manchester to tell Maria. Hilary's telephone in Switzerland was answered by Dougal Haston's widow, Annie. Betty Prentice, an old friend of us all, told Peter's mother in Bramhall and the local priest broke the news to the Taskers in Billingham.

Now, almost a year later, I can, I think, look back upon death in three ways. I mourn the loss of two close friends. I mourn, too, their great lost talents, singly and combined, their skills of climbing, writing, filming, humour, warmth and drive. Lastly, I question the nature of our journey – to venture with a small team on unknown ground on the highest mountain in the world. The outcome answers the question, 'Was it worth it?' It would not have been had we been able to peer even dimly into what was to happen. Since we are not granted this faculty I can only look back on the spirit of the venture.

I believe that with the mysteries of our personalities, our curious drives and our self-appointed goals, we could not have turned down this opportunity for fulfilment without denying ourselves a glimpse of the very meaning of existence. In time I expect we shall do the same again and be lured back perhaps by another Goddess Mother of the World.

Charles Clarke
May 1983

Peter Boardman and Joe Tasker were lost together on Chomolungma (Mount Everest). They were last seen on 17th May, 1982 at 8250 metres on the North East Ridge

Peter Boardman

1950–82

Peter David Boardman was born on Christmas Day 1950, the younger son of Alan and Dorothy Boardman of Bramhall, Stockport. He first went to Nevill Road County Primary School and then on to Stockport Grammar School in 1956. While there he began climbing, visiting the mountains of Corsica in 1964 and 1965. Here he first enjoyed the flavour of the wilderness, 'the freedom of moving, lightweight, through mountain country, carrying shelter, warmth, food and fuel on my back'. In 1966 he joined the Mynydd Climbing Club which then met in the Manchester Arms, Stockport. He began climbing seriously with Barry Monkman, a friend from school, and later with Dave Pownall. Once enrolled in the Mynydd he quickly became a highly competent rock climber, leading VS routes within a year on gritstone and Welsh and Lakeland crags. He visited the Swabian Alps in 1966, youth hostelling, and two years later went to the Pennine Alps to climb. He graduated quickly through Alpine classics to become a leading British Alpine mountaineer. He made the first British ascents of the North Face Direct of the Olan, the North Face of the Nesthorn and the North Face Direct of the Lauterbrunnen Breithorn.

From Stockport Grammar School he went to the University of Nottingham where he became President of the University Mountaineering Club. He took a degree in English, followed by a teaching diploma at University College of North Wales, Bangor, in 1973, where for a time he learnt Welsh. He was never to teach in any formal sense of the word but he joined Glenmore Lodge, Aviemore, in 1973 as an Instructor and gained the Mountain Guide Carnet in September 1977. He joined the British Mountaineering Council as National Officer in 1975 and despite little experience in the world of committees, he quickly mastered this demanding post, adding greatly to the BMC's contact with young climbers and climbing clubs, experience which would stand him in good stead when he was elected President of the Association of British Mountain Guides in 1979. His skill in negotiation and his knowledge of international mountaineering bureaucracy facilitated the entry of British Guides into the Union Internationale des Associations de Guides de Montagne. In January 1978, following the death of Dougal Haston in an avalanche, he was invited to take over the International School of Mountaineering in Leysin. As Director he helped continue the tradition of the school and found his metier as a guide and teacher of the sport he loved so much. Instructing climbing for Peter was never a necessary chore but a positive pleasure; he allowed his knowledge and affection to diffuse freely to those around him.

His first expedition was to Afghanistan in 1972, the University of Nottingham Hindu Kush Expedition, with Martin Wragg, Chris FitzHugh, Bill Church, Margaret and the late Oliver Stansfield, their baby Esther and Bob Watson. On this trip he demonstrated something of his own power – he was immensely strong and skilful, a man who valued speed as a means of safety. As a training climb his small party chose the North Face of Koh-i-Khaaik and followed this with the first ascent of Kohi-Mundi, a great achievement for a first expedition.

In 1974 he visited Alaska and with Roger O'Donovan made the first ascent of the South Face of Mount Dan Beard. Early in 1975 he went to the Caucasus and in July he left to go to the South West Face of Everest, the youngest member of the team and in many ways the least known. It was here that I first met him. Large expeditions were also a novel experience for him as an extract from his diary on the approach march shows: 'We round a corner and there is the British Raj in all its glory, neatly lined up erected tents, crowds kept at a distance, and we sit down at tables in the mess tent and are brought steaming kettles full of tea. For a mountaineer surely a Bonington Everest Expedition is one of the last great Imperial experiences that life can offer.' Peter was a diligent, disciplined member of the team, a little retiring on a sociable expedition. He was certainly one of the strongest members and this led to his selection for the second ascent of the South West Face, following Dougal Haston and Doug Scott. Peter was paired with the expedition Sirdar, Sherpa Pertemba and set off from Camp 6 in front of a second pair, Mick Burke and Martin Boysen. Martin turned back after a short distance with faulty oxygen equipment while Mick continued alone. Peter and Pertemba reached the summit of Everest in deteriorating weather at 1.40 p.m. on 26th September 1975. Peter was wearing, loyally, a Mynydd T-shirt for the summit photograph. With the conditions worsening rapidly they returned along the South East Ridge and to their amazement met Mick Burke ascending the ridge alone, about thirty metres below the summit. They exchanged a few words and agreed to meet up at the South Summit. Peter, despite deteriorating weather and poor visibility, insisted on waiting for over an hour and a half below the South Summit: in the storm that was to follow they were struck twice by avalanches while crossing the exposed slopes of the South West Face and struggled into Camp 6 in the dusk. Mick was never to be seen again.

In the months that followed it fell to Peter to record those moments many times, at lectures and at interviews. He did so with frankness and great sympathy, although it was obviously painful to him to recall what had been the momentous hours of his life.

After Everest '75, expeditions followed with frightening speed. In 1976 he visited the Polish High Tatra and later that year joined Joe Tasker for the West Wall of Changabang, the legendary climb which followed the lead of Joe and Dick Renshaw on Dunagiri a year earlier. Changabang was an example of meticulous forethought – for example the sleeve hammocks which were to dangle precariously on the face were first tested in a deep freeze – and much of the special equipment was designed and made by Mynydd members. This expedition, too, gave Peter a further share of tragedy, as Joe and he buried the bodies of four members of the American Dunagiri Expedition.

Peter had a companion as constant as his travels would permit for the last six years of his life. Acquaintance, girlfriend and finally wife, Hilary Collins had first met him as she took part in a course in Aviemore in 1974. In 1976, after Changabang she organised his first lecture, at Belper High School where she ran the School's Outdoor Activities Department. They climbed together shortly afterwards at the Torrs in New Mills (where Peter fell but was held by her) and later in the winter of 1976–7 in Torridon. There they planned a visit to New Guinea, Hilary then leaving for a post in Switzerland to teach in a private school. In 1977, unable to visit New Guinea, they climbed together on Mount Kenya (the second winter ascent of the Diamond Couloir) and Kilimanjaro. Peter was soon to follow Hilary to Switzerland, to Leysin, in 1978 when he took over the International School of Mountaineering. They were married in August 1980.

In 1978, by now firmly one of the most respected high-altitude mountaineers, he took part in the K2 Expedition led by Chris Bonington. Little was achieved; Nick Estcourt died in an avalanche early on the trip and the expedition was abandoned.

The following year was as full a climbing year as is possible. He spent Christmas 1978 in the Snow Mountains of New Guinea with Hilary, climbing the Carstenz Pyramid and Dugundugu. Peter spoke little about this small expedition, preferring perhaps to keep this tender memory to himself. 'Back from the Stone Age' in the New Year, he was ready to leave for Kangchenjunga in March with Joe, Doug Scott and Georges Bettembourg. They climbed the North Ridge of Kangchenjunga, reaching the summit without oxygen on 15th May. Returning for the Alpine summer season and guiding from Leysin, a further expedition was in preparation. Again a trip that was wholly in Peter's style – small, forceful and elegant to a mountain of mystery. This time it was Gauri Sankar in Nepal. Peter was openly disappointed that an American/Nepalese expedition, led by Al Read, had made the first ascent of the North Summit. The West Ridge to the virgin South Summit, looked hard and committing and with John Barry, Tim Leach and Guy Neidhardt (from Leysin), Peter left in September on the third extraordinary expedition of the year. This was as long, fine and intricate a ridge climb as has ever been done in the Himalaya, exposed for long sections and demanding sustained care. Despite John Barry falling from the crest and injuring his arm, the others reached the summit with Pemba Lama on 8th November.

For 1980 the unsettled score, K2, remained. It was not in Peter's nature to try to recreate a large expedition in the style of 1978. This trip was to be a foursome with Joe, Dick Renshaw and Doug Scott. Having attempted the West Ridge, they moved to the Abruzzi but once again the Savage Mountain struck, all but sweeping the expedition from the Abruzzi Spur in a succession of avalanches. They survived, reaching 7975 metres, but poor weather and exhaustion prevented a further attempt on the summit.

Mount Kongur followed in 1981, a large expedition by Peter's standards, but one which satisfied his keen interest in mountain exploration. He researched in great detail the history of climbing in Xinjiang and contributed important material to the expedition book. He reached the summit on 12th July with Chris Bonington, Al Rouse and Joe Tasker and narrowly escaped serious injury during an abseil near the top. A stone dislodged by his own abseil rope knocked him unconscious and he slid almost to the free end until, by chance, his thumb jammed in the descendeur.

Everest followed in March '82 and on this, our third expedition together, I sensed more of his feelings. Outwardly he was placid, apparently relaxed among high mountains with high risks. Growing to know him better I realised how aware he was of the dangers of his existence. He wore no blinkers about immortality and had no sense of fatalism – he wished to make sure he stayed alive. I thought he felt fear deeply but was somehow able to overcome it to achieve his extravagant climbing ambitions.

A further talent emerged through his climbing career – writing. He spoke and wrote well about Everest in 1975 but could not avoid the label of a successful new boy. Changabang, his first shared experience with Joe, seemed to me to be an event of such magnitude that *The Shining Mountain* leapt from him as part of all his inner experience, an outstanding document of endurance, pain, pleasure and a closeness to another human being. The success of the book was immediate in the climbing world and won him wider acclaim with the John Llewelyn Rhys Memorial Prize for literature in 1979.

Sacred Summits, published shortly after his death, described his climbing year of 1979, the trips to New Guinea, Kangchenjunga and Gauri Sankar. A book which captured both the variety and intensity of three very different expeditions, it will, I believe, be held in years to come among the greatest of climbing literature, for its merit rather than for its author's untimely end.

Although Peter's achievements with his partners will be recorded in the archives of mountaineering, it is his warmth, humanity and wisdom which will be so sorely missed by those of us who loved him. He did not agree with Howard Somervell's epitaph, 'There are few better deaths than to die in high endeavour'. Nor did Joe. And as I carved a headstone for their memorial in the Rongbuk Valley my only wish was for the last few moments of their lives to be unravelled.

Charles Clarke

Joe Tasker

1948–82

Joe was born in Hull in 1948 and five years later moved to Teeside where his father worked as a school caretaker until his retirement. Joe was one of ten children in a very close-knit family from which a strong sense of consideration and thoughtfulness for others seemed to develop. Several members of his family were usually at the airport when Joe left on an expedition or returned. Just before leaving on this last expedition to Everest Pete wondered whether Joe, noted for turning up at the last minute, would be on time to meet the press. 'He will be,' said someone else. 'Joe might keep the press of the world waiting but never his family.'

As the oldest son of a strongly Roman Catholic family, Joe was sent to Ushaw College at the age of thirteen. His seven years there were to have a lasting effect on him in many ways. It was there that he started climbing when he was fifteen, in a quarry behind the college, with the encouragement of Father Barker, one of the priests, and in the well-stocked library his imagination was fired by tales of epic adventures in the mountains. He was always grateful for the excellent education he had received and his amazing will power and stoicism may perhaps have been partly due to the somewhat spartan way of life and to the Jesuit ideals of spiritual development through self-denial. He started his training as a priest but at twenty realised that he did not have the vocation and decided to leave – the hardest decision of his life.

In complete contrast to his life at Ushaw was his first job – as a dustman. He enjoyed the hard physical labour and the friendly banter with his workmates and his forthright nature and ability to communicate with people from all walks of life broke down any barriers. He then went on to work in a quarry in the Lake District, where he was near the crags, for by now climbing had become a major part of his life. Feeling the lack of intellectual stimulation to which he had become accustomed at Ushaw, he decided to go to Manchester University to take a degree in sociology. The thin, fresh-faced youth looked the most unlikely of climbers but he soon made a big impression in the University Climbing Club with his keenness and drive, doing hard routes and often climbing solo. His climbing career almost came to an early end whilst he was soloing Three Pebble Slabs at Froggatt. His ancient pair of worn Kletterschuhe were not up to the thin friction and he fell, breaking his wrist so seriously that the specialist said the flexibility would be permanently impaired, curtailing his climbing. Never one to accept the hallowed words of experts without testing their veracity, Joe regarded this as a challenge and within a year was back climbing again with renewed enthusiasm and a brand new pair of EB's.

Whilst at university he was still finding his feet after so many years at the seminary and, although he was conscientious and absorbed by his studies, it was a time of experimentation and exploration. He was fascinated by the people living in their various ways, on the fringes of society, such as down-and-outs, alcoholics and gypsies. He had a deep concern for others and his understanding and genuine warm nature made him a very good friend. However, this side of him was not easily discernible as it was often hidden by an abrasive, hard shell. Despite his gregariousness and his ability as a raconteur he was also, in many ways, a very private person, sometimes appearing quite secretive and even enjoying creating a sense of mystery by making partial disclosures. During decision-making, whether personal or at a group level, he would not air his thoughts until he had fully mulled over the problem, often preferring to do so in solitude.

Although we were at the same university, we never climbed together during that period. Our first real encounter was in Chamonix in 1970 when, on a wet, dreary day, Joe's curly red head appeared through the door of my tent and he asked me if I fancied doing the North Face of the Dru. Having overcome his initial awe of the Alps, it being his second season, he seemed ready to tackle anything. It being my first, however, I was not and I demurred. The ice had been broken and we spent our first Alpine season together the following summer, climbing classic routes. The following year we again teamed up and developed a taste for North Faces. Joe really took to the mixed Alpine routes, relishing the insecure, delicate climbing. We were very different in personality and two seasons seemed enough but, nonetheless, we ended up climbing together again in 1973 after a chance meeting in Chamonix. We were both very ambitious and that season we climbed the Walker Spur, the Bonatti-Gobi Route on the Eckpfeiler Buttress, the North Face of the Nesthorn, the North Face of the Dent Blanche and the North Face of the Eiger.

Joe had got a good degree earlier that year but had decided not to settle into a career in order to be free to climb. At the end of the season all his money had gone and he decided to stay on in the Alps and find work in the Swiss vineyards in the autumn. He said that the penniless period between the end of the climbing season and starting work was one of the happiest times of his life. He survived on the refunds from empty wine bottles and on tins and packets of food left by departing climbers. He was able to relax and enjoy the mountains totally free from any cares about work, study or even climbing. After working in the vineyards he joined a group of young people at an archaeological site at Beaume in Switzerland and later on we had an abortive attempt at winter climbing in the Alps.

In the summer of 1974 we met in Chamonix or, as Joe put it, 'There was the unplanned but inevitable encounter with Dick, alone and looking for a partner. It doesn't do to fight one's fate and we arranged to climb together.' We did what Joe thought was one of the most memorable Alpine climbs – the East Face of the Grandes Jorasses, an intricate and demanding route. Joe had been stretched intellectually by academic life but the mountains provided the challenge to stretch mind and body to the full although I was continually amazed that someone who was so attached to his creature comforts should become involved in a sport which entailed so much physical hardship. At home he loved warmth and comfort: it was as though in times of plenty he was storing up an excess to help him through leaner times on the mountains. Frequently it seemed as though only his will power and determination drove his body on and it was not unusual to see him, at altitude, bent double over his ice axe racked by fits of coughing and spitting blood. The vast physical effort needed for mountaineering did not come easily but here, as in all his other activities, he had a powerful drive and restless energy.

Our ascent of the North Face of the Eiger in the winter of 1974–5 was a landmark in Joe's mountaineering career. It was an exhilarating climb and provided a stepping-stone to the Himalaya, giving us the necessary confidence to tackle a Himalayan peak as a two-man team. In 1975 we left Manchester in an overloaded Ford Escort van, our destination Dunagiri, a 7,000-metre peak in Northern India. It was an adventure from the start, fraught with problems and difficulties, but Joe seemed very much in control and methodically overcame one obstacle after another. He had the uncommon knack of going straight to the heart of a problem and solving it in the most expedient way. By September we were at 6,400 metres on the South Ridge but were insufficiently acclimatised, tired and, with few supplies and little fuel left, should have retreated. We both suppressed our doubts and fears, however, and this almost cost us our lives. We struggled on to the summit, leaving no resources for the descent which evolved into a four-day epic and left me with badly frostbitten fingers. Joe was becoming more at ease and more appreciative of the mountain environment and, having a natural eye for photography, was rapidly developing this talent and was able to record the mountains' changing moods. He was later to give a vivid description of the whole trip in his book, *Savage Arena*. In it he also describes the impression made on him by Changabang.

The days on Dunagiri were days of continual exposure to the subliminal presence of that stupendous mountain. It had been a thing of beauty beyond our reach, a wall of difficulty beyond our capabilities, it had been the obstacle which blocked the sun's warming rays in the early morning and the silent witness to my delirious wanderings.

He conceived the audacious idea of climbing the awesome West Wall as a two-man team. In Pete Boardman, Joe sensed a kindred spirit and the two of them combined to made a formidable driving force. Their success was a source of great delight to Joe, particularly as a number of established climbers had deemed the climb impossible, and it was the start of a brilliant partnership and a firm friendship. The rivalry between them was often evident, both of them setting very high standards in their goals which the other felt he had to attain or better. There was continual banter between them in which each tried to open up the chinks in the other's armour. Pete's presence seemed to induce in Joe a show of hardness and outrageous behaviour. They sometimes seemed like an old married couple but their banter would not have existed without a deep mutual respect and a strong affection.

In 1977 he attempted, without success, the North Ridge of Nuptse with Mike Covington and Doug Scott. That summer he went to the Alps but found that their allure was no more and thereafter he applied himself wholeheartedly to Himalayan expeditions. In 1978 he went with Chris Bonington's team to attempt the West Ridge of K2 and he witnessed the huge avalanche which swept his friend, Nick Estcourt, to his death, after which the expedition was abandoned. The following year, 1979, he went to Nepal with Doug Scott, Pete Boardman and Georges Bettembourg to attempt the North Ridge of Kangchenjunga (8598 metres) without oxygen. Until then Joe's highest climb had been to 7000 metres and to try to climb the third highest mountain in the world aroused in him many doubts about his ability to perform at altitude. Beneath Joe's appearance of confidence was a vulnerability which was very rarely expressed and which was counteracted by his ability to detach himself from his emotions. He proved himself capable of coping with the altitude and this exciting and successful ascent was, for Joe, an important personal achievement.

Frequent expeditions were taking their toll on his private life and his long absences and total involvement with mountaineering were too much for his personal relationships to withstand. In 1979 he began to organise an expedition to attempt, once again, the West Ridge of K2. At about this time he met Maria Coffey, who was to become a constant companion and a great source of strength to him. I had not climbed with Joe since 1975 but we had kept in touch and he had always been ready with his kind support. Valuing his friendships highly, he made great efforts to keep in touch with his many friends. Joe, Pete and I reached a height of 7975 metres on the Abruzzi Spur of K2 in very unsettled weather. It was one day's climbing to the summit from our tent, perched in a precarious position on a small ledge hacked out from a steep snow slope. During the night, after many hours of snowfall, an avalanche thundered down the slope, engulfing the tent, but miraculously not knocking it off the ledge. Joe was completely buried, Pete managed to extricate himself, dragged me out and we both dug out Joe. We had escaped death from the avalanche but there were a further three days of harrowing descent down slopes which after continual snowfall had become extremely avalanche-prone, with annihilation seeming imminent at each step. Back at Base Camp each of us individually decided to go back up for another try, and it was this decision which made Joe realise the depth of his commitment to mountaineering. It was an experience which had a profound effect on him.

Shortly after coming back from K2, Joe went off on an expedition to attempt a winter ascent of the West Ridge of Everest. Despite being still very weak and not having fully regained his weight, it was an example of his incredible will power that he was able to find the strength to apply himself fully to the task in hand. Conditions on the mountain were brutal and the cold more intense than he had ever experienced. They did not get to the top but it was an innovative step and showed the feasibility of winter climbing on the world's highest peaks. This expedition was the theme for Joe's first book, *Everest the Cruel Way*. It was an exciting account and revealed Joe's talent for writing. He wrote it in a very short time and under great pressure as he was also running a climbing shop and preparing for yet another expedition. He was also becoming more involved in filming and this was probably more suited to his gregarious nature.

In 1981, Pete and Joe were again together, with Chris Bonington and Alan Rouse, on the expedition to Mount Kongur.

The North East Ridge of Everest offered a double challenge for Joe – not only to climb it, but to film the entire expedition. He seemed to be living life at a cracking pace and sometimes felt frustration that there was not enough time to do all the things he wanted. He had just finished *Savage Arena* before leaving for Everest, and he completed his equipment appendix for the Kongur book just before we flew to Lhasa. There didn't seem to be enough hours in the day to pack everything in but it was evident that he was totally happy in what he was doing. At Base Camp there was the time and space to relax more fully and Joe amused us with funny stories and by appearing in the most bizarre clothes we had ever seen on an expedition. Life was never dull with him around and the constant jibes between him and Pete kept them on their toes and us entertained. I was very happy climbing with Joe: he had a fine judgement and I felt totally safe with him. He impressed us all with his professional attitude to filming and with his dedication, persevering in the foulest conditions. It was a bitter blow to me to have to leave the expedition after suffering a mild stroke and the night before I left everyone went off to their own tents after an early supper to write letters for me to take with me the following day. Joe had a heavy work-load to get through, completing his film reports as well as writing letters, but he must have sensed my desolation and, although it meant him working through most of the night, he stayed chatting with me and keeping me company for a couple of hours.

This thoughtfulness was typical of Joe and through his sometimes frenetic lifestyle there shone a very special warmth and vitality. He was an outstanding mountaineer and a very good friend.

Dick Renshaw

Both these obituaries also appear in the *Alpine Journal* 1983.

British Everest expedition 1982

CLIMBING TEAM
Peter Boardman
Chris Bonington
Dick Renshaw
Joe Tasker

SUPPORT TEAM
Charles Clarke
Adrian Gordon

TREKKING PARTY
David Newbigging
Carolyn Newbigging
Piers Brooke
Suzy Brooke
Robert Friend
Martin Henderson
Michael Jardine
David Livermore
Steven McCormick
Andrew Russell

CHINESE PERSONNEL
Chen Rongchang *Liaison officer*
Yu Bin *Interpreter*
Tang Huanzing *Trekkers' interpreter*
Wang Chouhai *Cook*
La Ba *Cook*
Cheng Wenxin *Jeep driver*
Dawa *Truck driver*

CO-ORDINATING OFFICE/SPONSORS
London
Martin Henderson
Philippa Stead
Elaine Edwards

Cumbria
Louise Wilson
Alison Lancaster
Norma Atherton

Hong Kong
T. T. Harley
P. A. Farnell-Watson

Peking
David Mathew
Alison Hardie
Peter Po

Canton
Rita Chan

Diary of events

1 March	Boardman, Bonington, Clarke, Renshaw, Tasker fly from Heathrow to Hong Kong.
4 March	Bonington and Clarke fly to Peking.
5 March	Boardman, Gordon, Renshaw, Tasker and trekkers fly to Chengdu.
6 March	Bonington, Clarke, Mathew fly from Peking to Chengdu.
8 March	All team fly from Chengdu to Lhasa.
9–16 March	Team drive to Base Camp.
17 March	Organising Base Camp.
18 March	At Base Camp.
19 March	Bonington, Renshaw, David Newbigging, Henderson, Jardine, Livermore and McCormick set out for East Rongbuk Glacier, camping at 5500m at junction of Central and East Rongbuk Glaciers.
	Boardman, Tasker, Friend, Russell, Piers and Suzy Brooke set out for Central Rongbuk Glacier and camp just below, by river.
	Clarke, Gordon and Carolyn Newbigging remain at Base.
20 March	East Rongbuk party reach Camp 1½ (5650m), a third of the way between Camp 1 and Camp 2.
	Central Rongbuk party walk up Central Glacier to approx. 5600m and return to their camp.
21 March	Bonington and Livermore return to Base Camp. Henderson, Jardine, McCormick, David Newbigging and Renshaw walk up East Rongbuk Glacier to 5850m and return to Camp 1½.
	Central Rongbuk party return to Base.
22 March	East Rongbuk party return to Base.
	American Everest team reach Base Camp.
23 March	Trekkers leave.
24 March	Team at Base.
25 March	Team go to Camp 1½.
26 March	Climbing team move to prewar Camp 2 (6000m) in 4 hours.
	Support team go short way and back to Camp 1½.
27 March	Climbing team go up to Advance Base (6400m) and return to prewar Camp 2.
	Support team go to level of Changtse Glacier and return to Base.
28 March	Climbing team return to Base (4 hours).
29 March	At Base.
30 March	At Base. American jeep goes out with mail.
	Yaks due but do not arrive.
	Americans move up to their Operational Base.

31 March	At Base. Bonington and Clarke visit nunnery.
	13 yaks plus 5 herders reach camp just below nunnery.
1 April	Yaks arrive at Base.
2 April	Team (less Renshaw waiting for mail) go to prewar Camp 1 with yaks.
3 April	Team go to prewar Camp 2. Renshaw at Base.
4 April	Team reach Advance Base. Bonington and Boardman stay. Clarke, Gordon and Tasker return to prewar Camp 2.
	Yaks return to prewar Camp 1. Renshaw walks from Base to Advance Base in 6 hours!
5 April	Bonington and Renshaw recce Raphu La and bottom of N.E. Ridge. Tasker moves to Advance Base.
	Support team return to Base.
6 April	Climbing team at Advance Base.
	Support team at Base.
7 April	Climbing team climb Ridge to site of First Snow Cave (6850m).
	Support team at Base. Discovery of prewar Everest memorial.
8 April	Climbing team at Advance Base making it windproof.
	Support team at Base.
9 April	Climbing team carries to First Snow Cave, starts digging and returns to Advance Base.
	Support team at Base.
10 April	Renshaw and Tasker move to First Snow Cave.
	Bonington and Boardman do a carry, returning to Advance Base.
	Support team to prewar Camp 1 with yaks.
11 April	Renshaw and Tasker push route short way beyond Point 7090 metres.
	Bonington and Boardman move up to First Snow Cave.
	Support team to prewar Camp 2.
12 April	Climbing team carry rope and push route to site of Second Snow Cave, 7256m.
	Support team to Advance Base.
13 April	Climbing team carry rope and food to Second Snow Cave.
	Support team at Advance Base. Yaks return.
14 April	Boardman, Renshaw and Tasker carry to Second Snow Cave and dig it out, then return to Advance Base.
	Bonington goes straight down to Advance Base.
	Support team at Advance Base.
15 April	Climbing team and support team at Advance Base.
16 April	Climbing team at Advance Base.
	Support team to Base.
17 April	Climbing team at Advance Base.
	Support team at Base.
18 April	Climbing team return to First Snow Cave.
	Support team at Base.
19 April	Climbing team carry to Second Snow Cave.
	Support team with yaks to prewar Camp 1.
20 April	Climbing team move to Second Snow Cave.
	Support team with yaks to Advance Base. Yaks stay up.

21 April	Bonington and Boardman climb First Buttress, reaching 7560m.
	Renshaw and Tasker snowproof Second Snow Cave.
	Support team returns to Base (because of theft).
22 April	Renshaw and Tasker climb Second Buttress, reaching 7640m.
	Bonington and Boardman follow, carrying rope.
	Support team at Base.
23 April	Climbing team return to Advance Base.
	Support team at Base.
24 April	Climbing team return to Base.
	Support team to camp at 6000 metres west of Rongbuk.
	American ski team arrive.
25 April	Climbing team at Base.
	Support team climb Point 6200, camp at Rongbuk.
26 April	Climbing team at Base.
	Support team return to Base.
27 April	All team at Base.
	Picnic at prewar Base Camp.
28 April	Climbing team at Base.
	Support team move to prewar Camp 1.
29 April	All team reach Advance Base.
30 April	Climbing team move to First Snow Cave.
	Support team at Advance Base.
1 May	Climbing team move to Second Snow Cave.
	Support team at Advance Base.
2 May	Boardman and Renshaw move up to Third Snow Cave at 7850m.
	Bonington and Tasker carry to Third Snow Cave.
	Support team camp on Kartaphu Glacier.
3 May	Boardman and Renshaw dig Third Snow Cave.
	Bonington and Tasker move up from Second to Third Snow Cave.
	Support team attempt Point 6919 and return to Advance Base.
4 May	Bonington and Boardman climb 4 rope lengths on First Pinnacle to 8100m, leaving fixed rope in place.
	Tasker carries rope to foot of First Pinnacle.
	Renshaw goes back to gear dump above Second Step.
	Climbing team return to Third Snow Cave.
	Support team at Advance Base.
5 May	Renshaw and Tasker force route on First Pinnacle to 8170m.
	Renshaw has minor stroke after leading very hard pitch.
	Boardman carries to high point and belays Tasker.
	Bonington carries to foot of First Pinnacle.
	Support team at Advance Base.
6 May	Climbing team return to Advance Base.
	Support team at Advance Base.
7 May	Team return to Base.
8 May	Team at Base.
9 May	Team at Base. Renshaw has second stroke.

10 May	Bonington, Boardman, Gordon and Tasker at Base.
	Clarke and Renshaw drive to Xigaze with Yu.
11 May	Bonington, Boardman, Gordon and Tasker at Base.
	Clarke and Renshaw reach Lhasa.
12 May	Bonington, Boardman, Gordon and Tasker at Base.
	Clarke and Renshaw fly to Chengdu.
13 May	Bonington, Boardman, Gordon and Tasker walk to Advance Base.
	Renshaw flies to Hong Kong.
	Clarke in Chengdu.
14 May	Boardman, Bonington, Gordon and Tasker at Advance Base.
	Clarke flies back to Lhasa.
15 May	Boardman and Tasker reach Second Snow Cave.
	Bonington and Gordon reach foot of North Col slopes.
	Clarke reaches Xigaze.
16 May	Boardman and Tasker reach Third Snow Cave.
	Bonington and Gordon at 6900m, just short of North Col.
	Last radio contact with Boardman and Tasker at 1800 hrs.
	Clarke reaches Base.
17 May	Boardman and Tasker last seen at 2100 hrs. at foot of Second Pinnacle at 8250m.
	Bonington and Gordon at Advance Base.
	Clarke at Base.
18 May	Bonington and Gordon reach and camp at previous high point at 6900m.
	Clarke walks to prewar Camp 1 with two Tibetans.
19 May	Bonington and Gordon reach North Col.
	Clarke reaches Advance Base with 2 Tibetans.
20 May	Bonington and Gordon on North Col.
	Clarke at Advance Base.
	2 Tibetans return to Base.
21 May	Bonington and Gordon join Clarke at Advance Base.
22 May	Bonington and Clarke return to Base, Bonington calling in at American Base.
	Gordon at Advance Base.
23 May	Bonington and Clarke at Base.
	Gordon at Advance Base.
24 May	Bonington and Clarke with Yu drive to Kharta. Meet American ski team.
	Gordon at Advance Base.
25 May	Bonington, Clarke, Ned Gillette, Jim Bridwell and Rick Barker reach yak pasture below Langma La (c.4850m) with 3 porters.
	Gordon at Advance Base.
26 May	Search team cross Langma La and camp beyond Karma Bridge at 4390m.
	Gordon at Advance Base.
	Yaks leave Base for prewar Camp 1.
27 May	Search team reach head of Karma Valley (American 1981 Base).

	Gordon at Advance Base.
	Yaks reach prewar Camp 2.
28 May	Search team examine Kangshung Face through telescope, then return to Karma Bridge.
	Yaks reach Advance Base, clear it, returning to Camp 1.
	Gordon walks to Base.
29–30 May	Search team return to Base.
31 May–1 June	Team at Base.
2–4 June	Bonington to Chengdu, breaks news by phone.
5–6 June	Clarke and Gordon to Lhasa.
	Bonington in Peking.
7 June	Bonington reaches Hong Kong.
8 June	Clarke and Gordon to Chengdu.
9 June	Clarke and Gordon reach Hong Kong.
10 June	Press conference in Hong Kong.
	Bonington and Clarke fly to London.
11 June	Bonington, Clarke and Renshaw attend London press conference.

A select bibliography

History and travel

Perceval Landon, *Lhasa* (2 vols), Hurst & Blackett, 1905.
L. Austine Waddell, *Lhasa and its Mysteries*, John Murray, 1905.
Fosco Maraini, *Secret Tibet*, Hutchinson, 1952.
Sir Charles Bell, *Tibet Past and Present*, Clarendon, 1924.
—*People of Tibet*, Clarendon, 1928.
—*Religion of Tibet*, Clarendon, 1931.
Sir Francis Younghusband, *The Epic of Mount Everest*, Edward Arnold, 1926.
Alan Winnington, *Tibet*, Lawrence & Wishart, 1957.
Peter Fleming, *Bayonets to Lhasa*, Hart-Davis, 1961.
Han Suyin, *Lhasa, the Open City*, Cape, 1977.
David Snellgrove and Hugh Richardson, *A Cultural History of Tibet*, reprinted by the Prajna Press, Boulder, Colorado, 1980.
Frank Steele, 'A Journey to Tibet and the Northern Side of Everest', *Journal of the Royal Society for Asian Affairs*, University of London, 1982.

Everest history

1921
Lieut. Col. Charles Howard-Bury and others, *Mount Everest, the Reconnaissance*, 1921, Edward Arnold, 1922.

1922
Brig. Gen. Hon. C. G. Bruce, *The Assault on Mount Everest 1922*, Edward Arnold, 1923.
Dr T. G. Longstaff, *This My Voyage*, John Murray, 1950.
George Ingle Finch, *The Making of a Mountaineer*, Arrowsmith, 1924.
John B. Noel, *Through Tibet to Everest*, Edward Arnold, 1927.
T. H. Somervell, *After Everest, the Experiences of a Mountaineer and Medical Missionary*, Hodder & Stoughton, 1936.

1924
Lieut. Col. E. F. Norton and others, *The Fight for Everest: 1924*, Edward Arnold, 1925.
John B. Noel, *op. cit.*
T. H. Somervell, *op. cit.*
D. Robertson, *George Mallory*, Faber & Faber, 1969.

1933
Hugh Ruttledge and others, *Everest 1933*, Hodder & Stoughton, 1934.
Hugh Boustead, *The Wind of Morning*, Chatto & Windus, 1971.
Frank Smythe, *Camp Six*, Hodder & Stoughton, 1937.
Eric Shipton, *Upon that Mountain*, Hodder & Stoughton, 1943.

1936
Hugh Ruttledge, *Everest, the Unfinished Adventure*, Hodder & Stoughton, 1937.
Frank Smythe, *op. cit.*
Eric Shipton, *op. cit.*

1938
H. W. Tilman, *Mount Everest 1938*, Cambridge University Press, 1948.

General climbing reference

Louis Baume, *Sivalaya: the 8000-metre peaks of the Himalaya*, Gastons-West Col.
Walt Unsworth, *Everest*, Allen Lane, 1981.
James Ramsey Ullman, *Kingdom of Adventure: Everest*, USA, 1948.

Chris Bonington, *Kongur, China's Elusive Summit*, Hodder & Stoughton, 1982.
Peter Boardman, *The Shining Mountain*, Hodder & Stoughton, 1978.
Peter Boardman, *Sacred Summits*, Hodder & Stoughton, 1982.
Charles Clarke, *Everest*, Sackett & Marshall, 1978.
Joe Tasker, *Everest, the Cruel Way*, Methuen, 1981.
Joe Tasker, *Savage Arena*, Methuen, 1982.

Picture credits

Index